Practical Navigation

Dag Pike

Imray Laurie Norie & Wilson

Published by
Imray, Laurie, Norie & Wilson Ltd
Wych House St Ives Cambridgeshire PE27 5BT England
☎ +44(0)1480 462114
Fax +44(0)1480 496109
Email ilnw@imray.com
www.imray.com
2015

All rights reserved. No part of this publication may be reproduced, transmitted or used in any form by any means – graphic, electronic or mechanical, including photocopying, recording, taping or information storage and retrieval systems or otherwise – without the prior permission of the publisher.

© Dag Pike 2015

Dag Pike has asserted his right under the Copyright, Designs and Patents Act 1988 to be identified as the author of this work.
A catalogue record for this book is available from the British Library.

ISBN 978 184623 681 5

CAUTION
Every effort has been made to ensure the accuracy of this book. It contains selected information and thus is not definitive and does not include all known information on the subject in hand; this is particularly relevant to the plans, which should not be used for navigation. The author believes that his selection is a useful aid to prudent navigation, but the safety of a vessel depends ultimately on the judgement of the navigator, who should assess all information, published or unpublished.

CORRECTIONAL SUPPLEMENTS
This pilot book will be amended at intervals by the issue of correctional supplements. These are published on the internet at www.imray.com and may be downloaded free of charge. Printed copies are also available on request from the publishers at the above address.

This work has been corrected to July 2015

Printed in the UK by CPI Anthony Rowe

Contents

1 Introduction *1*
2 Fixing the position *7*
3 Passage planning *17*
4 Harbour navigation *33*
5 Coastal navigation *46*
6 Collision avoidance *60*
7 Fog and night navigation *72*
8 Navigation under sail *84*
9 Navigation under power *96*
10 Coping with electronic failure *102*
11 Peripherals *110*
12 Phones tablets and computers *118*
13 The future *127*
14 Selecting equipment and installation *132*

Index *142*

1 Introduction

Background

Let's start with a bit of history. When I first went to sea more than 60 years ago we navigated across the oceans with just a compass, a chronometer and a sextant. Most of the time we got it right without too many disasters but the focus of the navigation was always on fixing the position. Making a landfall was a challenge, particularly when the visibility was poor. Even when navigating along coastlines using bearings from features on the shore, there was always an element of doubt and you had to make allowances for the uncertainty of the position. We would build in good safety margins to allow for this. A good navigator was one who was cautious, assessed the risks and took nothing for granted. Navigation was described as 'intelligent guesswork' and it was a long way from being an exact science.

Position fixing

Over the years, position fixing improved with the introduction of a variety of electronic systems. Radar was one of the first. It enabled sailors to get a fairly accurate fix by using a series of radar ranges instead of the manual compass bearings previously used, which would fix the position when you were close to land within a couple of hundred metres, if you were lucky. Early

The visual lookout is still a vital part of navigation

The original Decca Navigator system designed primarily for ships

radars were large and the first one that I went to sea with required you to walk inside it to switch it on. Small boat radars came years later and still required some skill from the navigator in order to identify the land features on the radar but they marked a considerable improvement. Then along came more advanced electronic systems such as Decca Navigator and Loran, which used signals from land-based transmitters. These produced a unique set of codes depending on your position that could then be plotted onto special charts overlaid with a plotting grid. The accuracy of these systems was pretty good, down to about 50 metres on a good day, but the level of precision was subject to variables including whether it was day or night, the distance from the transmitters and the weather conditions. Considerable user input was, therefore, still necessary to assess the accuracy. As with radar, small boat Decca and Loran receivers were eventually developed and gave the position in latitude and longitude, the first time that electronic positions had done this.

Satellites

The first satellite system was Transit. This gave a position anywhere in the world but only at intervals of 30 to 40 minutes. It was not, therefore, too much use for coastal navigation or fast boats but it helped to put some certainty into the position when making a landfall.

GPS

Finally, we arrive at where we are today with GPS which, from a navigator's point of view, is like the Holy Grail. When it was first introduced, the accuracy of GPS was understated because it was primarily a military system, and the authorities did not want ordinary users to have access to the high accuracy positions that were possible. Eventually the US military relented and today GPS will fix your position with an accuracy of around 20 metres, or even less if you have one of the more sophisticated systems. It works 24 hours a day and the position information is continuous and unaffected by the weather. What more could a navigator ask for?

GPS has transformed the face of navigation, enabling sailors to know exactly where they are at all times, whether in the harbour or the middle of the ocean. As a result, the emphasis of navigation has changed completely; you can now focus on where you are going rather than trying to find out where you are. For a navigator brought up the hard way this is a tremendous step forward. The accuracy and reliability of GPS positioning has made the electronic chart a viable proposition and navigation today can be as straightforward as plotting a suitable route on the electronic chart and making sure that the boat follows the line on the screen. If desired, you could even set the autopilot to follow the line and change course when required, largely automating the navigation and allowing you to sit back, relax and enjoy the sun.

Before GPS you had the excitement of making a landfall after an overnight passage, perhaps picking up the faint loom of a lighthouse in the far distance, and then as the sun rose, losing the lighthouse to see it replaced by the hard edged outline of the land. These could be exciting and satisfying moments for a navigator but they were often combined with a definite element of stress. The advent of GPS has taken some of the challenge and drama out of navigation but that's not a bad thing.

The strong degree of certainty that GPS has brought to navigation has changed it from 'intelligent guesswork' into a much more exact science and has added a level of precision to position fixing and landfalls that was previously unimaginable. Despite this, navigation remains far from simple. There remains the complex matter of collision avoidance as other craft get in your way and sailors must also consider the possibility of the GPS failing or becoming unreliable.

Accuracy and reliability

I will look at the question of GPS reliability in Chapter 10 but if you are a prudent navigator then you will not rely entirely on electronic systems to see you safely to your destination. There is always the possibility of a failure in the electrical supply to electronic equipment and on many boats the equipment itself is operating in the harsh environment of an open cockpit which is certainly not conducive to reliability. I was brought up to never completely trust electronic systems and over the years I have experienced many failures. I, therefore, have an inherent mistrust of electronics and always try to have a back-up plan to cope with failures.

You may have been brought up with electronics as an integral part of your daily life in the form of mobile phones, TV and

Visual navigation marks are still important

INTRODUCTION

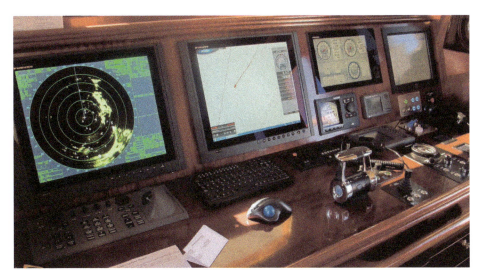

Full sized electronic displays on a large yacht

music systems. Nowadays, cars and even boats are fully electronic so your trust in these systems is entrenched. But it's vital to remember that although in daily life many electrical failings are little more than an inconvenience, at sea they could land you in serious trouble.

Then there is the human element. In the early days, you still had to assess the accuracy of the information received and there was always a strong element of negotiation when fixing the position and extracting information from the radar and other systems. Because modern electronics present you with so much precise information for navigation it's hard to question its quality and accuracy. When a position is given to four decimal places of a degree, which is less than a metre, what grounds do you have to argue? What you need to do is look as much at what the electronics do NOT say as at what they do.

The basics of navigation have not changed and you still need to question the quality and accuracy of the information you are being presented with. It is too easy to rely on navigational electronics and become occupied by other distractions whilst boating at sea but safe navigation is a full time job and it needs to remain your principle focus.

Lights are a valuable guide into harbour

GPS accuracy may be quite adequate for coastal navigation but is it good enough for the close quarters navigation required when entering harbour? Are the charts that you are using accurate enough to show the position of all the potential dangers around you? Is the accuracy of the GPS position enticing you to reduce your safety margins and perhaps navigate closer to rocks and shoals? On a single-engined boat do you have enough of a safety margin to cope if the engine fails? On a sailboat do you have adequate margins to cope if the wind freshens or a rope breaks? This is where your judgement comes into play. It is, therefore,

PRACTICAL NAVIGATION *3*

INTRODUCTION

The view from the bridge - what the big ship navigator sees

vital to understand the basics so that you can make a safe passage. We will look at this in more detail in Chapter 3, Passage Planning.

Visual navigation

One of the basics of navigation is to keep a check on your position by all possible means. Visual navigation is, therefore, a key backup for electronics. The world outside the wheelhouse or cockpit is both interesting and informative and can offer any number of clues about your location as well as improving safety. Learn to judge distances at sea by estimating the distance from a feature on shore and then measuring it on the electronic chart. Use your echo sounder to make sure that the depth conforms to what the chart shows. Set a course so that you pass close to buoys or other navigation marks to give you a visual fix. All of these techniques will help you to relate what the electronic information is telling you to what you see outside in the real world. It is important to appreciate that if you get things wrong with electronic navigation, you could be in serious danger.

Three screens

Today we have what are known as the 'three screens' for navigation: the electronic chart, the radar and the windscreen. The view beyond the windscreen is still a vital part of navigation and you ignore it at your peril. Electronic systems may do your navigation for you, they may help with collision avoidance, but they are unlikely to detect floating debris or small fishing marks that

The author navigates his way out of harbour

4 PRACTICAL NAVIGATION

INTRODUCTION

Only visual navigation is likely to pick up floating debris like this

may be in your path and which could damage your boat. Even on big ships with multiple electronic screens the view from the window is still vital.

Paper charts

Always have paper charts on board. Apart from providing a good back-up if electronic systems do fail, the paper chart is a mine of information about the real world outside the cockpit or wheelhouse. It usually contains considerably more information on land features than can ever be found on electronic charts which tend to be simplified to avoid overloading the relatively small display screen. The land features shown on paper charts, such as hills and cliffs, may have an effect on the strength and direction of the wind coming off the land and can be useful tools in helping to identify where you are. Paper charts can also show what material the seabed consists of; useful when anchoring. As such, I find the paper chart to be a wonderful tool when passage planning. On some boats it may be a challenge to find space to lay out a paper chart but it is worthwhile making room in order to gain a wider picture of your cruising area.

Electronic systems

Electronic navigation systems can offer a vast array of features. Information can be displayed in many different ways, with satellite overlays, horizontal views of the coastline and even images of the underwater contours. Manufacturers exploit every possible combination of display and information in what is seen as an attempt to enhance the possibilities of the equipment. However, much of this information can be

The paper chart can provide a check on the electronic systems

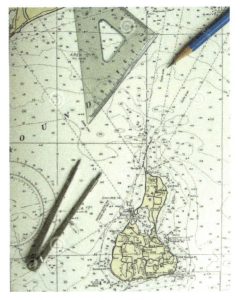

Traditional paper chart navigation where you have to get fully involved in the work

superfluous to practical navigation. It can prove to be a distraction and I am a great believer in keeping things as simple as possible. Switching to alternative displays and trying to find information in the comprehensive menu options can take your eye off the basic navigation information so, if you can, try to keep things simple. Complicated controls can sometimes make it challenging just to switch from daytime to night-time lighting modes and I have found equipment that required five push-button strikes and the assistance of the handbook before this could be achieved. Simplicity is a great asset when you are trying to use

PRACTICAL NAVIGATION 5

INTRODUCTION

Relying on prayer will only get you so far with navigation

electronic equipment during a wild night at sea or when you are challenged by fog conditions. Even on big ships where navigation is done in the comfort of a warm wheelhouse, there are calls to have a button on the sophisticated electronic navigation system which, when pressed, will restore the display to a basic navigation scenario that any competent navigator can understand.

Equipment

This book will focus on the practical aspects of navigation:

- how to select the right equipment for the job
- how to install it to use it to maximum advantage
- how to use it in a variety of navigation scenarios

On some boats you may not have a lot of choice in the first two of these aspects because the builder has chosen and installed the equipment before you have a say in the matter. In this case the focus will be on how to use the equipment and how to use the wealth of information provided to navigate in a safe and effective manner. Most of the dedicated electronic equipment available has been designed for use in the marine environment but we are now seeing electronic devices that you use in everyday life, such as smartphones and tablets, being made navigation capable. The lines between navigating on land and at sea are becoming blurred and we will look at the pros and cons of this and how to use the equipment effectively.

Weather

The weather is an important part of navigation at sea yet it tends to be treated as a separate subject. Whether under power or sail, the weather so often dictates what you can or cannot do on a passage and the wind direction and strength, in particular, will tend to rule your available actions and navigation decisions. Electronic systems may have taken a lot of the guesswork out of navigation but forecasting winds and sea conditions still requires your input.

Electronics can come to your aid here as well, enabling you to keep up to date with weather changes, but remember that weather forecasts are predictions and not an exact account of what will happen to the weather. We all have our stories of inaccurate weather forecasts and their considerable impact on our voyages.

Navigation is an evolving science, one where the basics remain the same but the techniques and technology are changing. You have probably spent some considerable time learning how to drive your boat and mastering the techniques of efficient sailing. It is the same with navigation, it can be both challenging and fun and you can take pride in getting it right. We will look at how to use the information provided by electronic systems in an effective way so that you're able to get your boat from A to B in a safe and seamanlike manner.

2 Fixing the position

Global Positioning System

Establishing your position is a pre-requisite for any navigation. Your position gives you the starting point, the reference to work out where you are going from and where you are in relation to any surrounding dangers. As I said at the start, fixing your position used to be the major challenge for navigators but today GPS does the job for you. The Global Positioning System (GPS) can fix your position anywhere in the world to an accuracy of around 20 metres or better. However if you are going to use GPS positions intelligently you do need to understand the system and any situations where it could go wrong or give you false information. With such an all-encompassing position fixing system it can be too easy to take its accuracy for granted.

Satellites

GPS is an amazing piece of technology. There are 24 active satellites, plus a few spares, circling above the Earth at around 10,000 miles. They are on pre-determined orbits and the whole constellation is designed to ensure that you have at least four satellites in view at any one time. You will probably see several more but this is the minimum number needed to ensure a three-dimensional fix. At sea you are not too concerned with height so a two-dimensional fix is adequate for navigation.

The accurate position of the satellites is known and each transmits signals that are picked up by the receiver on board your boat. Without going into too much detail:

- The system measures the time it takes for these signals to travel from the satellite to your location, this time can then be translated into a range from each satellite to give a fix. Much like when travelling along a coastline at sea, where if you have three ranges from fixed points then you know your position.

- The system translates this fix into a latitude and longitude position that can then be plotted automatically on the electronic chart or manually onto a paper chart.

GPS error sources		
Error source	**Typical range error**	**DPGS (code) range error <100km ref - remote**
SV clock	1M	
SV Ephemeris	1M	
Selective availability	10M	
Troposphere	1M	
Ionosphere	10M	
Pseudo-range noise	1M	1M
Receiver noise	1M	1M
Multipath	0·5M	0·5M
RMS error	15M	1·6M
Error *PDOP=4	60M	6M
*PDOP = Position Dilution of Precision (3-D) 4·0 is typical		

FIXING THE POSITION

The initial electronic display showing the wide choice of information available

- The whole process is fully automated and provides a position that is accurate for most practical sea navigation purposes.
- The timing of the signal coming from the satellite is measured in millionths of a second and the distance involved is thousands of miles.

The satellite positions must be known with extreme accuracy because your position will depend on this accuracy. It is a tribute to the development of the system that it can be packaged into a small handheld unit and produce such accurate positions.

External factors

Because of its phenomenal accuracy and reliability, it is very hard for the navigator at sea to question this system, yet it is vulnerable to outside influences and you must be aware of these.

The signal coming from the satellite is extremely weak; when it leaves the satellite it is around 50-watts and has to travel 10,000 miles or more, losing power along the way. Imagine trying to view a 50-watt light bulb from 10,000 miles away; it's not hard to imagine that the signal can be influenced by external factors. Just passing through the

FIXING THE POSITION

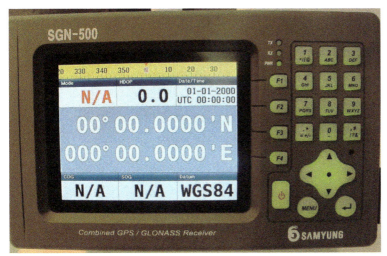

Position accuracy is shown to 4 decimal places which gives an unrealistic indication of normal GPS accuracy

Earth's atmosphere can affect the signal. If a satellite is located close to your horizon, the signal has a longer journey through the atmosphere than one from a satellite that is higher in the sky and this can affect its accuracy.

Your receiver will automatically select the best satellites available so you should not have to worry about this too much, but if you are interested you can select the satellite page on your display to see which ones are being used out of all those that are available. Intense solar flare activity emanating from the surface of the sun can also affect the signals, or even shut the system down, but this is closely monitored and not likely to be a cause for too much concern.

GPS blocking and jamming

The frequencies used for the GPS system are remote from most others in order to avoid interference, but a powerful transmitter in your vicinity could block the GPS signals simply by swamping the ether. I have come across this in the vicinity of Rapallo in Italy where there is a powerful air beacon on the land close by to guide planes into Genoa airport. This can make it hard to pick up any GPS signals in that very localised area. Sophisticated receivers are designed to be capable of operating in areas where there is 'noisy' radio frequency interference but this is not always the case with the cheaper GPS receivers that can be found in equipment such as mobile phones and other handheld units.

Trying to pass too close to a navigation mark is not a good idea

A small unit that is connected into the GPS antenna can reduce the risk of GPS jamming

PRACTICAL NAVIGATION

FIXING THE POSITION

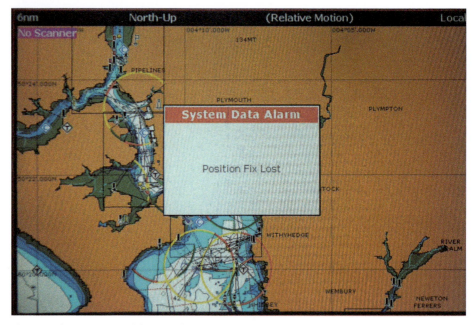

The sort of display you might see when the GPS signal is lost

More sinister is the possibility that the GPS signals could be vulnerable to jamming. Cheap GPS jammers are readily available on the internet at low cost and most of these have a short range because they are primarily designed to cut out tracking devices on trucks or cars where the drivers do not want their location to be known. It has been reported that this type of GPS jamming or blocking is detected eight to ten times a day in the Southampton port area so, although it is short range jamming, it could affect GPS reception for boat navigators in port areas.

Of greater concern are longer-range GPS jammers with the potential to cover several kilometres. They are becoming more readily available and could be used to jam the GPS signal over a considerable area. It is not hard to imagine that a terrorist organisation with a powerful jammer of this type could disrupt the very weak GPS signal over a sensitive shipping or aircraft area and trials have confirmed that this could be a real threat.

Even more sinister is GPS spoofing, where a false signal more powerful than the GPS signal is sent out which, rather than simply blocking the GPS signal, alters it and gives false positioning information which then appears on your receiver. With jamming you are likely to get a warning on the display that the signal has been lost but with spoofing this will not happen. You may still be able to detect spoofing; a sudden jump in the displayed position should act as a warning, however, more sophisticated spoofing tests have shown that with clever spoofing techniques a vessel can be guided off course without the crew becoming aware of what is happening. This type of spoofing is much more likely to be aimed at shipping targets than yachts but could be aimed at all the vessels in a local area so the risk remains.

Alternative satellite systems

So here you are, presented with the most incredible position fixing system that effectively solves all your navigation problems, only to find that it can be vulnerable to outside influences. This demonstrates that for all its benefits you should not take GPS positions for granted and as always with navigation you need to check your position by other means as often as possible. There are other satellite

FIXING THE POSITION

navigation systems such as the Russian Glonass system, the European Galileo system and the Chinese Compass with more to follow as each country seeks to develop its own system. However, all of these systems operate on frequencies that are close to those of GPS so they are could be just as vulnerable as GPS to jamming and spoofing and it is likely that if one goes down, they will all go down, because of the closeness of the frequencies.

Technical issues

Then there is the system itself. GPS is such a complex system that I am always surprised that it has such an amazing reliability record. There are enough back-up features built into it to ensure that its reliability is excellent but the risk of failure remains. The equivalent Russian Glonass system went out of action for 13 hours at one point and there has been no explanation forthcoming of why it failed for this considerable period of time.

GPS antenna

High quality GPS antenna often have some anti-jamming features built into them. These are usually filters that tend to narrow down the frequencies that the antenna can receive and can filter out what are likely to be the less focussed frequencies of a jammer. The military cannot afford to have their GPS signals jammed by an enemy and have, therefore, developed some very sophisticated anti-jamming devices, which are built into their equipment. Some of the techniques used in these military systems are now available on the commercial market and it is possible obtain dedicated GPS antenna filters for fitting to the widely available retail electronic GPS receivers. Using one of these should help to eliminate the worry of GPS jamming but you have to decide whether the potential risks justify the cost and complication of one of these units. If you understand the basics of traditional navigation it shouldn't be necessary to

A radar display also showing all the GPS data

purchase a filter, but if you rely solely on GPS then it could be a useful investment.

An exposed GPS antenna can be sensitive to ice build up if you are operating in very cold conditions. This would usually be the result of spray landing on the very cold surface of the antenna and acting as a barrier between the signal and the antenna. It is possible to avoid this problem with a heated antenna but the issue is likely to be more relevant to commercial vessels than to those used for pleasure because one does not tend to go to sea when it is bitterly cold. Furthermore, the GPS antenna purpose-designed for marine systems are improving all the time. Many are now capable of receiving signals inside a wheelhouse rather than having to be mounted in an exposed position outside. Some modern chart plotters have the GPS antenna incorporated into the dashboard display unit, improving reliability by reducing connections and external wiring.

Other position fixing systems

Before satellite navigation became a reality, there were terrestrial electronic navigation systems such as Decca Navigator and Loran.

With these you fixed your position from signals sent out from terrestrial transmitters and plotted these on charts overlaid with a special grid. The accuracy was adequate, maybe in the order of 100 to 200 metres, and later versions produced a latitude and longitude readout to facilitate plotting on normal charts.

Now, an advanced system called eLoran or Enhanced Loran, is being proposed to act as a back-up and a means of checking GPS positions. Trial eLoran systems are already up and running in Europe and the option is being considered in the US.

The fact that investment in a back-up system is considered necessary demonstrates that the authorities are concerned about the vulnerability of GPS as land, sea and air transport becomes increasingly reliant on it. There is no real need to be pessimistic about the availability of GPS signals as they are probably available 99.99% of the time, which for most boaters is more than adequate. That said, the possibility of failure, however likely, makes it sensible to have a back up in place.

Contingency planning

I have yet to experience any cases of jamming and spoofing and it may be that the risks to GPS are exaggerated. More likely

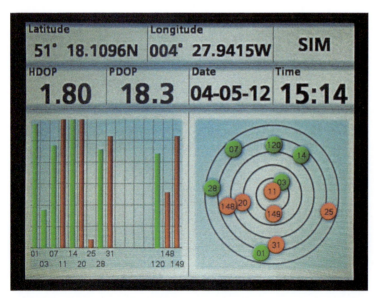

A GPS display showing the satellites in use and the accuracy expected (PDOP)

FIXING THE POSITION

issues may be the loss of the power supply to the electronics on board or a fault in your GPS antenna and its connections. The power supply scenario might be sidestepped by having portable GPS or chart plotting systems with built-in batteries on board (your smartphone or tablet might meet this requirement), but if you do find that the main GPS has gone down and you have no back up, what do you do?

We will look at this in detail in Chapter 11 but suffice to say if you are running on autopilot, keep this running because it will at least take you on to your next waypoint, which will hopefully have something to identify it visually, such as a buoy or a headland. This is the time when experience with visual navigation can be valuable, and visual navigation is always a good way to check GPS navigation anyway. There are so many clues to be found through the wheelhouse windows or looking around you from the cockpit. Rather than blindly sticking to the GPS, take in these visual clues to your location not only as a check but also as a means of navigating should your GPS let you down. We have come to rely on GPS to such an extent that many navigators would be lost without it. Perhaps it could be a good idea to switch off your GPS and other electronics once in a while and practise visual navigation, which, after all, was the primary means of navigating as recently as 20 or 30 years ago and is still effective.

Position lines

Fixing your position by visual means used to mainly involve taking bearings of fixed objects with the hand-bearing compass and plotting them on the chart. If possible you took bearings from three objects on shore, not unlike the GPS which obtains ranges from three satellites. Most yachts today are unlikely to have a hand-bearing compass on board but you can still get a position line just by observation. A position line is a single line on the chart along which your position must lie and that position line could be a range or a bearing. Where two position lines cross you have a position fix but even with just one position line you can at least know that there are many areas on the chart where you cannot be. A position line narrows down the options considerably and there are many ways to get one.

With practice, you can estimate your distance off the shore or a headland and this can give you a position line. It may not be very accurate but, if you practise estimating distances and then checking them against the electronics, you will soon get better at it. A more accurate position line can be established when two objects on the shore are in line so that you can get what is known as a transit bearing. This is very reliable and gives you a good position line.

Transit bearings

To plot the transit line on the chart, the objects used must already be marked on the chart. This can narrow down the options but they do make a good check, and these transit bearings are used in quite a few harbours to give a position line that will show that you are in the deep water channel of the harbour.

Leading lights and soundings

Leading lights do the same thing at night and are used in many ports and harbours as a good guide to supplement the buoyage. Another way to establish a position line is by using soundings. If the sounder says that the depth is 10 metres, you can't be in deeper or shallower water, provided of course that your sounder is set up properly and you have allowed for the rise and fall of the tides.

Buoys

The easiest type of visual fix is with a buoy. When you are passage planning, it can help if you set a route that passes fairly close to buoys, when possible, so that you have this visual check. We will look at this in more detail in the next chapter, Passage Planning.

Radar position fixing

Radar can also be used for position fixing as you can measure both range and bearing of an object from the radar. Radar ranges will always be more accurate than radar bearings because with the latter you have to take into

PRACTICAL NAVIGATION *13*

FIXING THE POSITION

A paper chart can often provide a better solution when navigating in harbours

account the course you are steering, assuming that the radar is being used in the normal head-up mode on the display. By applying the true course that you are steering to the relative bearing taken from the radar, you end up with a true bearing that you can plot on the chart. Using radar ranges, the position is fixed in much the same way as when using the ranges from the satellites, although with radar ranges you have to plot them manually and ideally you need at least three ranges to able to plot the position with confidence. Ranges also need to be taken from objects that you can identify both on the paper chart and on the radar.

GPS accuracy

Having said all this about fixing your position visually, GPS is, of course, going to rule your position fixing most of the time, so just how accurate is it?

The GPS receiver is measuring time in nanoseconds and in most cases you can expect the accuracy to be in the order of 15 to 20 metres. It can be even more accurate than this; it all depends on the quality of the receiver and its ability to process the signals, the location of the satellites in relation to the receiver, and the atmospheric conditions. Most GPS receivers for marine use are good quality, much better than for instance, the one which you may have in your phone, and they should have multiple channels enabling them to receive signals from several satellites simultaneously rather than sequentially.

In theory, you can expect to get accuracies of between 15 and 20 metres 95 percent of the time but what about that other five percent? Well, unless you are navigating to close margins, the lower accuracy of that five percent will average itself out and you will not notice it. A common scenario in which you may find yourself position fixing to close margins is when navigating in harbours using GPS. In this situation the margin for error can be considerably reduced. We will look at this in more detail in Chapter 5.

Do remember that a possible error in the

FIXING THE POSITION

position could be in any direction so in effect the error between any two subsequent positions could be double the actual error. Try to visualise the position given by the GPS as a circle of position on the chart rather than just a single dot. This will help you to appreciate that there can be varying degrees of accuracy.

World Geodetic System 1984

A position given by the GPS is no use to you until it is plotted on a chart and you can see where you are in relation to the land and other features. The electronic chart does this automatically, which is one of its bonuses, but with a paper chart you have to plot the position manually. In both cases, this is where things can get complicated because the GPS uses a chart datum based on the World Geodetic System 1984 (WGS84) and it is important that the chart you are using, whether it is electronic or paper is using the same system. It took quite a few years for the change in the chart datum to be switched to WGS84 but today you should be fairly comfortable that the charts you use are on this GPS datum.

The details on the chart will all be referenced to this datum but, if you are sailing in some more remote parts of the world, the surveys on which the original charts were based may not have been as accurate as we expect today and you may find that the GPS position is some way out compared with what is shown on the chart.

This is likely to apply more to paper charts than to electronic ones but it is something to bear in mind if you are navigating to close margins using GPS.

Remember also that information shown on both types of chart will never be fully up to date. There is always a time lag between the surveys being carried out and their data appearing on a chart. This can be particularly relevant to harbour charts where the information shown regarding depths in the main channels may be up to date to allow for the safe navigation of shipping but outside the main channels the harbour authorities may be less meticulous about the survey accuracy. In harbours the GPS positions may be accurate enough but channels and buoy positions can change at short notice and catch you unawares.

GPS receivers

This may all sound a bit frightening but in reality you can use GPS to navigate with confidence in open waters, just don't expect it to take you precisely into your marina berth in thick fog! Remember that the receiver you have on board is measuring the position from the location of the GPS antenna and even this might be some distance from the wheelhouse or cockpit on larger craft. The antenna should be located in a clear position where it can pick up signals from all around the horizon without interference and it should be located clear of transmitting antenna linked to any radios on board.

On many good quality GPS receivers and/or chart plotters you can find the expected accuracy of the GPS position hidden away in the menus. This accuracy is based on the positions of the satellites used and their relative location to give a good crossing angle of the fix. It is labelled HDOP (Horizontal Dilution of Position) but don't take this accuracy figure as absolute because it is only an estimation based on the location of satellites and doesn't take into account the variable atmospheric conditions and other factors that can affect the signal.

Latitude and longitude

Some confusion can arise from the way that the positions are shown on the display as a latitude and longitude. Most manufacturers now use degrees, minutes and decimals of minutes to show a position but some might use seconds, which are a sixtieth of a minute rather than decimals of minutes. For chart plotters, the plotting of the position is done automatically but, if you are trying to transfer the position shown on the GPS to the paper chart, the lack of a seconds read-out can make things more difficult. Charts still mainly use the latitude and longitude scales in the original degrees, minutes and

FIXING THE POSITION

Fixing the position with radar can be challenging unless you can identify the land features

seconds format so you need to do a bit of juggling if you are trying to plot a position shown in decimals of a minute. It could be the same when a position is transmitted over the radio, such as in the case of a distress signal position, and you need to be clear about what format is being used. On most electronic displays the position is shown with three decimal places of a minute accuracy and this can give a false impression of the actual accuracy. Three decimal places of a minute mean that the position is being displayed to an accuracy of about two metres; a degree of accuracy unlikely to be achieved in practice. One or two manufacturers even take the position to four decimal places, which brings it down to the centimetres level; something impossible to achieve with a standard GPS receiver but that undoubtedly looks good and could impress the uninformed! Use a bit of caution when presented with such high accuracy levels.

Summary

Nowadays, therefore, it is possible to know where you are to a degree of accuracy and reliability that would have been unheard of 30 years ago and you can go off and start to navigate with a considerable degree of confidence.

Please do not be too put off by all this talk of the potential shortcomings of GPS. It is a wonderful system and has transformed navigation at sea. It promises nearly everything that a navigator could dream of: good accuracy day and night, worldwide coverage, and continuous automatic position fixing.

Most of the time it fulfils these promises but if you are a sensible and cautious navigator, you will treat GPS with respect and, as with most navigation information, try to verify what it is saying all the time. After all, if you get it wrong, it could be your life at stake.

3 Passage planning

Writing a passage plan

Passage planning is a legal requirement before you set off to sea. It makes sense because it ensures that you have a good idea of where you are going and the sort of conditions and challenges that you might experience along the way, as well a sense of the options should things go wrong. In its simplest form, passage planning is where you just plan your route and check the tides, the weather and the alternative ports along the way before you set off. This might work for a quick day trip but if you are off on a cruise then there are really three stages to passage planning. The first is to look at the overall route of the cruise and where you plan to go during the week or two that you have available. Secondly you do more detailed passage planning for each leg of the cruise a day or two before you set out on that leg. Finally there are the last minute checks that you need to do such as getting an up-to-date weather forecast an hour or two before leaving and assessing what the sea conditions and the visibility might be like along the route.

A boat (as opposed to a ship) may not be expected to have a written passage plan, but if you don't then you could find it challenging to show that you did actually develop a passage plan. It can sound onerous to write everything down but that will help to make sure that you have ticked all the boxes of the requirements that are detailed later.

Advance planning

The general planning of your cruise can be done over the winter long before you leave. Spreading out the paper chart and dreaming of where you plan to go may sound like a romantic view but this armchair planning can bring a lot of pleasure and anticipation. The joy of working on a paper chart, as opposed to on a computer, is that you have a much

> ### LEGAL REQUIREMENTS FOR PASSAGE PLANNING
>
> Prior to proceeding to sea the Master shall ensure that the intended voyage has been planned using the appropriate nautical charts and nautical publications for the area concerned, taking into account the guidelines and recommendations developed by the organisation.
>
> The voyage plan shall identify a route which:
>
> Takes into account any relevant 'ships' routeing system and ensures sufficient sea room for the safe passage of the ship throughout the voyage
>
> Anticipates all known navigation hazards and adverse weather conditions
>
> Takes into account the marine environmental protection measures that apply and avoids as far as possible, actions and activities which could cause damage to the environment.
>
> *There is a third paragraph that says that it is the Master that is responsible and that owners and charterers cannot interfere with that responsibility, but on a small boat you are likely to be the Master and the owner and everything else in between.*

wider view of the area that you plan to cruise. In my opinion, you can get a much better feel for the layout of the sea and the land; it is easier to visualise the cruising area and to see the beginning and the end of a day's cruise on the one sheet of paper.

Tide races off headlands need to be considered when passage planning

PASSAGE PLANNING

Charts

Paper charts are a masterpiece of graphic display with so much information and detail contained on one sheet of paper. As you should be carrying paper charts on board as a back up to electronic systems there is no reason not to use them at the planning stage of a cruise too. Whichever system you feel most comfortable with, paper or electronic charts, it is the planning that is important so that you have thought through all the options and reduced the chance of nasty surprises. It is much easier to plan and plot things either ashore or when in harbour rather than trying to work things out when the boat is tossing around at sea. When I was racing I used to plan a whole variety of route options to allow for the possibility of changing conditions and situations. During the actual race you might only use perhaps 30 or 40% of these options but you had to do the whole lot because you did not know which you would want. You should adopt the same approach when cruising.

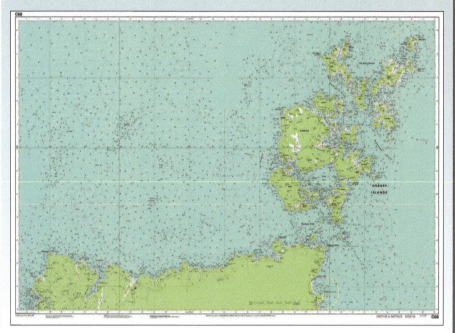

Paper charts are a masterpiece of graphic display

Timing

You may have a week or two for your cruise but so often have to be back in your home port by a certain day. For this, your planning will need to build in some sort of reserve of time so that in the event of adverse winds and conditions you will not find yourself under pressure to get back and perhaps take unnecessary risks to meet that return deadline. One of the major reasons why people get into trouble at sea is that they feel that they are under a time pressure to complete a passage and so take risks when the weather and sea conditions suggest that staying put might be the prudent thing to do. You can get a pretty good idea of what the weather will be like three or four days ahead using weather forecasts so, on a week's cruise you will be able to get a fair idea of what the future holds when you are halfway through your cruise. This is the time when you can continue as planned or whether you think you ought to cut things short and head towards home.

Routes

If you plan a cruise that is a simple out and back route along the same coast then you will find yourself at the furthest distance from your home port just at the point when you will be getting those reliable forecasts for the last few days and thinking about the return trip. However it is at this point you will have run out of many of your options because there is only one way to get home which is back the way you came and you need the full three days to do that. A simple out and back cruise of this type has its attractions but it does not allow you any flexibility or room to negotiate with the weather if things turn sour. You tend to feel under more and more pressure the further you get from home so this will probably not be a relaxing approach to cruising either. There are two alternatives to this dilemma, firstly plan a triangular cruise that will allow you to cut off one of the corners of the triangle if you need to save a day or to make up time from any delays. In this way you can build flexibility into your cruising plans and be more relaxed about the future. The other option is to plan a lay day somewhere along the cruise where instead of continuing along the coast you might stay in harbour and explore a river or estuary in the tender or just have a day off relaxing in harbour and enjoying a stroll ashore. This lay day could then be used to catch up on time in the cruise if the weather does not look like cooperating.

Most out and back cruises take place along a coastline and it is easy to see the attraction of this. You are not faced with any long sea passages where you have nowhere to run to if things go wrong, because with coastal cruising there is usually a convenient harbour close at hand if you change you mind or you are not comfortable with the conditions. With the sort of triangular cruising suggested you can still include some coastal cruising if you plan things carefully. A triangular cruise might involve leaving from the south coast of England and heading across the Channel to France. Then you cruise along the French coast, which leaves you with the option of then of heading back home across the Channel early if the forecast looks like turning sour. You could do the same in the Irish Sea, and in the Mediterranean there are many fascinating islands that you could include on your itinerary which would then allow you to vary your plans according to the weather. For the alternative of building in a day in harbour there are so many interesting places up rivers or estuaries along many coastlines that can be used as a day diversion from coastal cruising.

Marinas and anchorages

You may choose to cruise from marina to marina, and this is the choice of many motor cruiser owners where it can be easier to keep to a cruising timetable because you are less dependent on the wind for propulsion. Marina cruising usually means booking ahead in order to be sure of a berth at busy times which will take some of the flexibility out of the cruising plan, but marina cruising offers the convenience of a 'step ashore' berth and plug in facilities like power and water. At busy times it may be easier to cancel a booking if plans change than trying to book a berth at short notice. The options are to arrive on spec and hope or to plan overnight stops at anchor in quiet spots, although quiet anchorages are becoming increasingly hard to find in many popular cruising regions. Anchoring at a stopover point is real cruising where the boat really becomes your self-sufficient home. It does mean being totally self-contained, doing your cooking, having adequate water on board and on modern boats perhaps having to run the generator to get the power for the cooking or battery charging. You still need to plan for this because you will have to ensure that you have adequate food and water on board because you can't easily nip ashore for more.

Your initial cruise planning should also take into account the capabilities of your boat and your crew. The comfortable cruising yacht will be the choice of most cruising sailors with performance craft at one end of the spectrum and rugged blue

WEATHER CHECKLIST

Radio forecasts
The VHF radio will give forecasts possibly four times a day but these tend to be quite general.

Internet forecasts
There is a huge amount of weather information on the internet and a good source is www.weathercharts.org

Local weather
The local weather conditions and cloud formations can give you a good idea of the progress of weather fronts.

Conditions at destination
Before departure, check the conditions at your destination, particularly in a fast changing weather situation.

Fine tuning
You can fine tune the weather forecast as regards timing forecast by relating what you see outside in the clouds, which can indicate the arrival of a frontal system

Land and tide influences
When cruising along a coastline the topography of the land can influence the wind considerably whilst tidal conditions can have a significant effect on the sea conditions.

Safety margins
Remember that the forecast of winds is only a forecast and winds can be stronger that those forecast particularly in local areas so allow a safety margin when assessing the forecast.

Decision making
You need to take many factors into account when deciding if conditions are suitable for a passage: forecast winds, local topography, tidal conditions, harbour entrances and shallow water and how they all interact.

---

water cruisers at the other. This applies to both sail and power and with a well found cruising yacht you can cope with adverse weather in confidence, but if you are just cruising as a couple as the crew on board then you might want to consider a more cautious approach. This should be reflected in your planning.

Again in planning you need to consider where your cruising pleasure will come from. Is the time spent at sea? Is it the pleasure of days exploring a new port? Or perhaps it is the simple pleasure of successfully completing a passage. A cruise is rarely as simple as just a line of the chart from A to B so when you do your early planning consider what you hope to achieve. Also consider where you can stock up with fuel and water and other stores. There is a lot to think about.

Weather forecasts

Once this early passage planning is done and a sort of cruising plan emerges you can put your charts away until a few days before departure when you will be able to feed information about the forecast weather and what the tides will be doing into the plan. This is where the serious navigating starts and at this stage you should be able to fine-tune the programme and have a better sense of what is possible. In a sailboat it can be helpful to know if there will be headwinds on the way that can make for a longer passage tacking into the wind. The same can happen with a motor cruiser where you might need to moderate the speed in head seas in the interests of comfort. Advance weather forecasts are therefore vital. The internet is a rich source of information about the weather, with forecasts stretching ten days ahead. See www.weathercharts.org where you will find weather and wave forecast charts to meet most of your requirements and cruising areas. You do need to take any long-range weather forecast as a guide because no forecast for ten days ahead is going to be completely precise. Weather patterns will normally be quite accurate but may not necessarily keep to the time schedule that is forecast for several days ahead. Long-range forecasts should be able to give you a general idea of which direction the wind will be coming from and that can be a great help. You could always reverse the direction of your cruise as a result, so that with luck and a bit of planning the wind will be from a favourable direction and you can take maximum advantage of the conditions in order make life on board more comfortable. Start taking the weather forecasts from say about five days before you leave and you will be able to see the pattern of the lows and highs and their associated frontal systems developing, so you will have a good feel for the weather situation and the possible changes that can be expected. Weather can play such an important part in navigation when cruising or even when just making a one-day passage and whilst you cannot change the weather you can negotiate with it in terms of your direction of travel and your timing.

Tides and distances

Settle on a sensible mileage plan for each day so that the cruise does not tax your resources. Tidal flow can have a considerable effect on the progress of slower boats and of course sailboats have to be conscious of

OTHER INFORMATION SOURCES

In addition to weather information, the internet is an invaluable source of other information for the cruising sailor.

Google Earth

Lets you view images of the places that you intend to visit, which will give you a much better idea of what to expect as you enter an unknown harbour and what you might encounter when you get there.

Electronic chart systems

Many have graphic or satellite overlays with pictures like those on Google Earth

Harbour and marina websites

Most harbours and marinas have a website with information about berthing, contacts, refuelling etc.

Pilot guides

Can also be a great source of information and can give a tantalising glimpse of what a place is like to visit.

Take note that none of these resources is likely to be fully up-to-date and should be viewed with caution, but can provide a very useful guide. They tend to be written by people who have visited and have experience of using harbours and marinas in the locality.

You can get a variety of displays for harbour approaches on electronic chart systems

PASSAGE PLANNING

Check the route carefully for dangers before passing close inshore

wind direction and strength. With any head winds you will be covering a greater distance when tacking. Even motor cruisers can be adverse to head winds and seas, which can make life on board very uncomfortable.

So how do you plan your cruise to take maximum advantage of the tides if that is what you want to do? The answer to this is to work backwards and rather than schedule a time that you want to leave harbour, work out the time when you want to be, say, rounding a significant headland to get the most favourable tide. From that point you can work backwards to see what time you will need to leave harbour to be at the headland on time to catch the best of the tides. With a sailboat you need to work out in advance the departure time for various boat speeds, say anything from 3 to 6 knots, and then you can pick the departure time to suit the wind and conditions on the day. Of course working like this could lead to leaving harbour at some rather antisocial times but to a large degree you can dictate the terms, balancing early starts against the tidal and weather advantages and you can vary elements in your short term planning before you leave.

We are talking here about negotiating with the tide around just a single headland but of course there may be several of these to negotiate with during a day's passage, and there is little chance that you will be able to get the tide right at all of them. However there is usually an optimum time for departure to get maximum advantage from the tide during the course of a day's passage. Tidal flow information can be found in the traditional booklets and on paper charts but increasingly, this information is now to be found superimposed onto electronic charts in real time, which enables you to see at a glance what you can expect. Studying the tidal charts and establishing what the tide will be doing will be an important part of any passage planning and there are computer programs that can do this for you and suggest the optimum time to leave.

A satellite overlay can sometimes provide a clearer picture of the topography

22 PRACTICAL NAVIGATION

PASSAGE PLANNING

PASSAGE PLANNING – PAPER CHARTS

Draw proposed route

Mark the waypoints along the route you want to follow and then connect with a pencil line. Check that these lines pass safely away from any dangers, using larger scale charts if necessary.

Measure courses and distances for route

Measure the courses and distances along the lines you have drawn and mark these on the chart so that you have a full picture of where you are going and the courses to steer for future reference.

Look for significant marks/lights along the route

Check the proposed route for any buoys, significant buildings, features and/or lights that will help you to identify visually where you are. On a night passage, write the characteristics of any flashing lights for quick reference.

Look for alternative courses for the route

An alternative course might take you inside a bay to avoid head seas and winds or you may want to tack offshore. You might want to have an alternative course to pass close to a buoy if the visibility is poor.

Find courses and distances for these alternatives

Write down the courses and distances of these alternatives so that again, you have a quick reference.

Find times of high and low water

The time of high and/or low water at ports on the route can be written on the chart for quick and easy reference.

Identify tidal streams

Check out what the tidal flow will be doing along your route and in particular check any cross tides that will have to be allowed for when setting a course.

Obtain weather forecasts

Weather forecasts will help you to determine the best routes by establishing what the wind will be doing. Both sail and power boats want to avoid head winds if possible and you can establish which areas might be sheltered from the forecast wind. The forecast should also show if the wind will be veering or backing as you make progress along the route.

Look for alternative ports

Passage planning requires you to establish alternative ports along the route for use if conditions deteriorate or you have problems. Accessibility and tidal conditions at these alternatives should be checked and you need a contingency plan in case things go wrong. You also need to make sure that someone on shore knows your plans and intentions so that if you do not turn up as expected then they can inform the authorities.

Be aware of the limitations of both boat and crew on the proposed passage.

Checking the details

In this second stage of passage planning you will have all the courses and distances plotted along the route, perhaps on the paper chart, perhaps on the electronic systems or best of all, on both. If you do plot your route with a series of waypoints on the electronic chart then go back over the route in detail with the chart expanded to a large scale because, on vector-based systems, the information on electronic charts tends to be selective according to scale. The chart scale you use for the general plotting may not show up all the detail on the longer ranges and it can be easy to miss something like an off-lying rock on these longer range charts. To a certain extent the same applies to the paper chart and you should use the most detailed chart where possible to check the route you are planning to avoid any nasty surprises. One of the yachts in the challenging Volvo Ocean Race circumnavigation failed to use a detailed chart and plotted a route that went over a shoal area without realising it. That is the sort of high profile grounding that you want to avoid!

PRACTICAL NAVIGATION

PASSAGE PLANNING

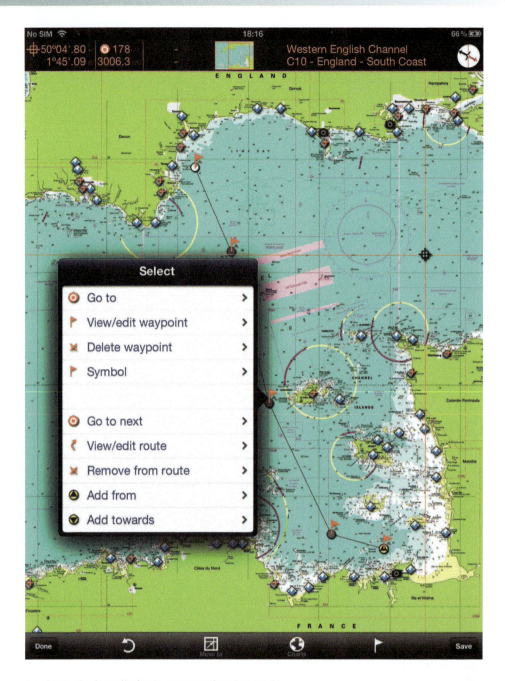

An electronic chart display in passage planning mode

PASSAGE PLANNING - ELECTRONIC CHARTS

Open the chart plotter to the largest size

You want the maximum size screen picture when plotting your route. Some small plotters can be challenging when trying to plot a route so get rid of any surplus information on the display.

Open a chart that will show the beginning and end of the proposed voyage

This display will give you an idea of where the voyage will take you and what the alternatives might be.

Remove any old routes or waypoints so that you start with a clear display

De-clutter the display so that there will not be any confusion when you come to plot the route in detail. However you may be using a previous route so of course you will leave that one on the display.

If you are offered a choice then select Rhumb Line from the Great Circle/Rhumb Line options

Most routes will follow the rhumb line between waypoints which is the straight line joining the two points. A great circle route will only be used on longer passage of over 300M or so, and then mainly on E/W courses.

Insert the start waypoint, zooming into the chart to obtain a suitable scale that shows adequate detail

Your starting waypoint is likely to be just outside a harbour entrance although you can also plot the route from inside the harbour if there is a long entrance channel.

Plot the waypoints along the proposed course around headlands and/or close to buoys etc

These waypoints need to be chosen with some care allowing safety margins so that you pass clear of headlands and offlying shoals and rocks.

Plot the finish waypoint on a suitable scale chart

Like that at the start, the finish waypoint one can be off a harbour entrance or even take you into the harbour channels depending on the type of harbour. Try to find a location on the chart where the shore will be clearly identifiable for when you make the change from electronic navigation to visual harbour navigation.

Go back to the start waypoint and track along the route at a large scale to ensure that it does not pass close to or over any dangers and that there are adequate safety margins

Remember that not all dangers will be shown on smaller scale charts.

Check that there is adequate distance off headlands

These are the points where you tend to come closest to the land so make sure there is adequate clearance to allow for the wind and/or the tide setting you in towards the land.

When satisfied that the route is safe, save it to the plotter memory

Once you have checked the proposed route in detail, save it to the plotter memory so that it can be called up on departure. There will be another chance to check it just before you leave.

Check tidal information

Make a note of the times of high and low water along the proposed route and what the tidal streams will be doing. Some plotters have tidal information available and show the tidal streams on the display.

If you can, check for any chart updates and for any navigation warnings

Try to get the latest information about any changes in the chart displayed. You may be able to get an update for the chart or check Navtex information.

Identify alternative ports

Look for alternative ports along the route and check for accessibility regarding tides etc.

PASSAGE PLANNING

Safety margins

This detail-checking of the route will also enable you to check what safety margins you have built in. Safety margins are mainly established in the distance off that you will pass any dangers, so that if something does go wrong on board you do have a bit of time available to sort it out before you drift inshore. It is always nice to pass close to the land or other features from a tourist point of view but you need to balance this against the need for safety. Passing about a mile off would be an adequate safety margin in most cases but think about allowing more if the wind is blowing onshore. Other factors that might make you consider going further

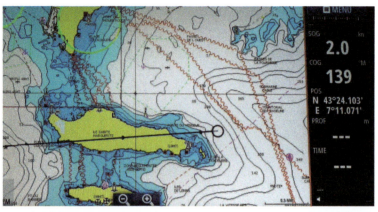

You need to consider the safety margins when passing between islands like this

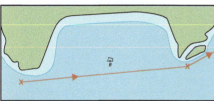
The initial course

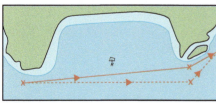
Modifying the course to allow more clearance

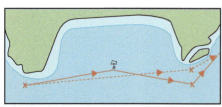
2nd modification to pass close to the buoy

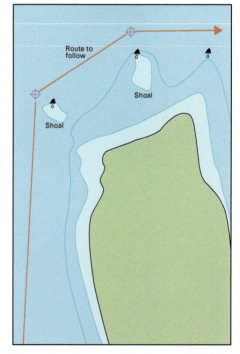

Carefully check the course that you plot on the chart to make sure that you adequate clearance at danger points and possibly to make visual sightings of navigation marks

When choosing waypoints along a route it is better to set them some distance away rather than through the actual position of a mark

PASSAGE PLANNING

offshore can be tidal races, such as those around some headlands, and of course, off-lying shoals or rocks. Taking channels inside islands and shoals is always a possibility to shorten a voyage and to add interest to the cruise and you must balance this against the need for safety margins. This is one of the main responsibilities that you undertake with passage planning and having a 'what if' mentality can be useful when trying to balance the risks against the expediency. There are no hard and fast rules and this is where experience and judgement have to be used to ensure a safe passage.

Should things go wrong or the weather turn out to be worse than predicted then you may need or want to curtail the passage. This is why in your passage planning you need to identify alternative ports. Obviously if you are making an open sea crossing, say across the English Channel or the North Sea, there will not be much in the way of alternative ports available en-route but along a coastline there could be quite a few. As part of your passage planning, check to see if these ports have any tidal restrictions or if the entrance could be dangerous in certain conditions of wind and tide thus restricting

Sighting a buoy can give you a reassuring visual fix when on passage

availability. Also remember that the port that you have just left could be one of these alternatives and if you get out to sea at the start of the passage and find the conditions worse than you expected you can always turn back. At least the port you have just left will be a known quantity.

You need to expand the scale considerably when navigating in waters like this

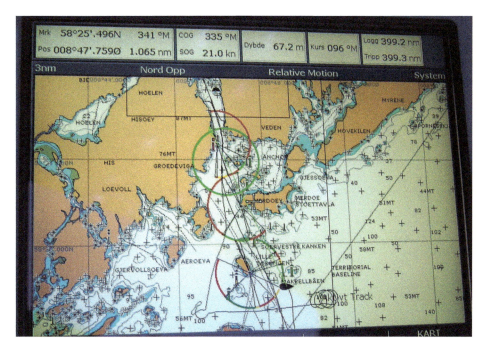

PRACTICAL NAVIGATION 27

PASSAGE PLANNING

ALTERNATIVE PORTS CHECKLIST

Check the chart for alternatives

Both paper and electronic charts will show any alternative ports along a proposed route. You are required to have alternative ports in your passage plan but make sure that they are accessible.

Facilities in alternatives

Research the facilities that are available in alternative ports such as marinas, moorings, fuel supplies etc before deciding whether they are a suitable alternative.

The port you have just left

When considering alternative ports always remember that the one you have just left should be added to the list. This will be the logical choice if you find that the conditions outside are not comfortable for the passage you had in mind.

Any tidal or weather restrictions

When electing alternative ports some may not be accessible because of adverse tidal or wind conditions. A strong wind blowing onshore can create very challenging sea conditions in some harbour entrances.

Enough fuel on board to reach them

Calculate the distance to any alternative port, particularly if it is beyond your destination port, to ensure that you have enough fuel plus a reserve to get there. You may turn towards an alternative if you have a problem on one engine so can you reach the alternative on the remaining engine?

Courses and distances on charts

Draw courses and distances from a close waypoint to the alternative ports so that you have a ready reference if an emergency forces you to aim for the alternative.

Tidal information

A set of tide tables gives you the times of high and low waters in various ports around the country and also the actual height of the tide on a particular day. From that information you can work out just what the height of the tide might be at the port you are interested in and the time you anticipate being there.

However, you can get the same information in a more useable form on the internet. This is as a graph that on the vertical scale shows the height of the tide and on the horizontal scale shows the time and date so you get a harmonic curve showing the ups and downs of the tide. From this it is easy to find the time and date that interests you, the height of the tide at that time and whether the tide is rising or falling. You can usually get this information for a week or so ahead, and it can be a good idea to print this out for relevant ports so that you have an easy reference to see tidal heights when you need them.

The passage plan

You will have:

- identified the prevailing tides and weather
- identified alternative ports of refuge
- built in adequate safety margins such as distance off dangers, potential areas of breaking waves and busy shipping lanes.

Passage planning is a requirement to promote safety so that you have a good idea of what you are going into and you have planned for alternatives if things don't work out as planned. Much of this planning you will probably not need but when you leave you do not know which part this might be so you need to do it all.

Electronic systems

Like everything else to do with navigation, passage-planning software has becoming increasingly sophisticated. One electronic chart even has the option to enter the starting point and the proposed destination point and the system works out the whole course for you. In my opinion that is perhaps a step too

Arrival in harbour at the end of a successful passage

28 PRACTICAL NAVIGATION

PASSAGE PLANNING

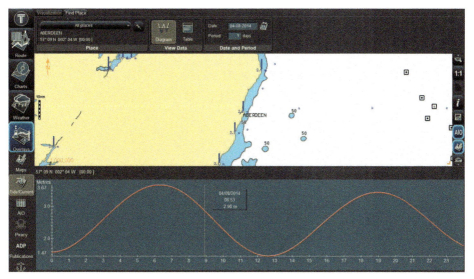

The vertical scale shows the height of the tide and on the horizontal scale shows the time and date so you get a harmonic curve showing the ups and downs of the tide

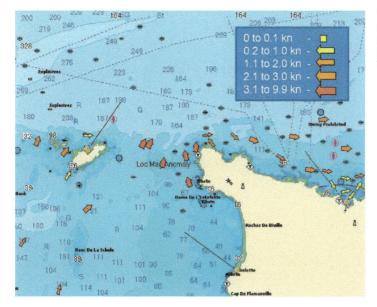

Tidal arrows showing the direction and strength of the tide in real time

far because you want to know what criteria have been used in establishing and plotting that course, what safe distances away from dangers and what safe depths have been used, what deviations are possible so that you can get a visual confirmation of your position, etc. You can feed in some of these factors such as the minimum depth and distances off before the electronics do the rest, but letting the electronics do the rest makes me nervous. Such an automatic system will offer you a selection of waypoints to follow but if you do go down this route then a very detailed check on what is on offer is vital to confirm that it is actually a safe route to follow. Even when you select the waypoints yourself on an electronic chart then you need to do this detailed check of the route to ensure that it is indeed a safe

PASSAGE PLANNING

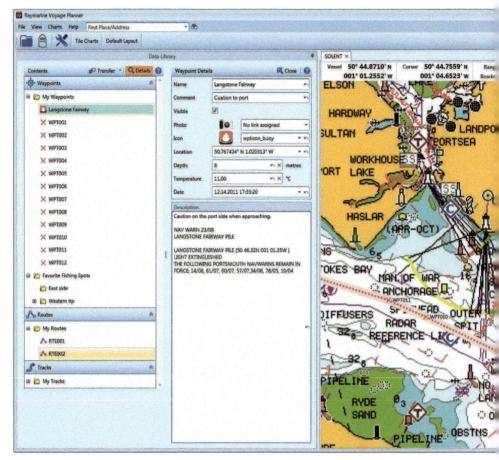

Detailed passage information with dedicated planning software which needs checking carefully before use

route to follow. Some systems will warn you if the proposed route crosses land or other dangers but don't rely on it.

Planning on paper

If you are plotting on a paper chart then you will need to measure the courses and distance from waypoint to waypoint so that you have them available. On the electronic chart this will be done for you and the route will show as a series of courses and distances. In an ideal world you should write these down as your passage plan just in case the electronics go down but for most navigators these days the reliability of the electronic system is such that this is never done and you put your faith fully in the electronics.

If your planned passage extends into night time there are additional things you want to add in such as light characteristics which you might want to add to the paper chart in large letters or write down from the electronic chart for reference but we will look at this in more detail in the Night Navigation chapter. Certainly in adverse conditions such as poor visibility and night navigation the planning becomes more important because it frees you up to concentrate on the essential lookout.

PASSAGE PLANNING

When passage planning keep your crew in the picture

Weather

Weather plays such an important part in any voyage you make at sea. It can determine the courses you take, the availability of alternative ports and the level of enjoyment and comfort on board. It is easy to take the weather forecasts literally and believe them implicitly, but you are able to have a strong input into the weather forecasts by studying the weather patterns for a few days before

A route plotted through an inside channel

PASSAGE PLANNING

you leave and looking at the prevailing weather in your locality. Then you will be able to relate changes that you can see visually with what the forecast is saying and put a much better timing to forecast changes.

Last minute checks

The final stage of your passage planning will be done just before departure when you update the weather forecast, check for any restrictions in the harbour of departure such as large ship movements, make sure that your radio is working and your safety equipment in good order, and the boat is secure for going to sea. Have you told the crew what you are planning so that they know what is involved and have you informed someone on shore what your plans are and what is the approximate timing for the voyage?

Heading out to sea is not just a question of preparation of the navigation such as the passage planning; it can also entail a considerable shift in responsibilities. On shore your actions are governed by a whole host of rules and regulations, some local, some national, which take a lot of responsibility off your shoulders as long as you comply. Out at sea, you are in charge and you are responsible. As far as regulation is concerned you need to comply with the Colregs and you must not discharge oil into the water but there are surprisingly few other regulations you need to conform to. This means that you have to set the standards and you have to take responsibility for your safety and that of your crew, which is why passage planning is an important feature of your safety regime.

The ball is firmly in your court out at sea and officially you are 'Master unto God' and take the blame if things go wrong. No wonder they call it 'Shaking off the Shackles of the Shore' when you head out to sea and leave the land behind.

FUEL AND PROVISIONING

Fuel is another consideration in your planning particularly on a motor cruiser. It is pretty obvious that you need enough fuel on board to complete the passage comfortably and a good reserve should be at least 20% to allow for the increased consumption that might occur with headwinds and seas.

You should have a good idea of the consumption of your yacht at various speeds and your calculations should take into account the worst-case scenario. On a twin-engined boat if one engine fails and you have to run on the remaining one you could find you could find that the consumption per mile increases.

Even on a sailboat fuel should be part of your passage planning because you may have problems with your sails and have to complete the passage under power.

The same could apply to fresh water and stores if you are planning a long voyage extending for days rather than hours and in this case you might want to consider one of the electronic weather routing programs that can optimise the route to follow according to the forecast winds ahead and your sailing polar diagram.

Of course you can do this manually but the electronic system can take a lot of the guesswork out of the equation and can be remarkably accurate.

4 Harbour navigation

A confusion of marks in a harbour entrance

There can be a significant difference between coastal and harbour navigation.

For coastal navigation you will most likely be using electronic systems with visual navigation as the back up.

For harbour navigation it tends to be the reverse and visual navigation takes priority.

Of course electronic systems can be used in harbours and in some circumstances they can be very useful but you need to understand their limitations in confined waters. In harbours there is little margin for error and you can find yourself working to much closer limits than you would ever dream of when offshore. When you enter harbour you not only encounter waters and surroundings that may be new to you but you enter an area where the land is closing in and close encounters in confined spaces become the norm.

Entering harbour can be an exciting time but also one of increased tensions. It can be exhilarating watching a whole new harbour open up before you, almost like the thrill of discovery, but with it comes a degree of uncertainty and to make it work you do need to do a bit of planning in advance. When you are cruising, planning ahead is the key to making most things happen in a reasonably ordered and controlled way, as we have seen under Passage Planning. This preparatory work comes into its own when you are entering a new and unknown harbour.

Before departure

Any voyage does, of course, begin by leaving harbour, so I will start by looking at the practicalities of this. Naturally, this phase brings its own tensions, as you wonder what it will be like outside and what the voyage will bring. However, leaving is usually an easy operation as far as navigation is concerned; you start off in the confines of a marina or moorings but things open up as the harbour expands. There can be a great temptation to just jump on board, fire up the engine and let go the ropes. I have often seen boats leave harbour with this casual approach and get out to sea only to have to stop and stow loose bits of gear, try to get some useful information out of the electronics, get the radar running, work out the navigation scenario and prepare the boat for the sometimes lively motion that you can find out at sea. Although it can seem tedious when you want to get out into the open sea and begin the voyage in earnest, it is much easier to carry out those tasks in harbour before you leave.

PRACTICAL NAVIGATION *33*

HARBOUR NAVIGATION

NAVIGATION CHECKLIST

Waypoints entered and electronics programmed

Setting up your electronic chart system before you leave means that when you reach the harbour entrance you are ready to navigate along the chosen route.

Radar on and set to appropriate range

If the radar is set up and ready to use when you leave, it will be readily available if you need it in a hurry, perhaps if the visibility outside is poor. The 1M range might be best for harbour use and the 3M may be suitable when you are outside.

Paper charts annotated and ready for use

You should carry paper charts and they should have the courses and distances marked on them so they are ready for use if the GPS or other equipment fails. Updating the current position on the paper chart is a good idea.

Departure chart displayed and ready for use

Unless you feel you need the electronic chart for navigating within the harbour, set up the display at the range of detail that you will need once you are outside.

Echo sounder on and working

The echo sounder can be a valuable check when you are navigating within the shallow waters of a harbour.

Call harbour or marina authorities on VHF radio

You may be required to give the harbour or marina authorities a call on the VHF radio before you leave. This is a good chance to check that the radio is working.

VHF radio on and checked – set to harbour frequency

If you have the VHF radio set up on the harbour working frequency, you should be able to monitor the movements of shipping within the harbour and plan your timing accordingly. Put the radio on scan so that it will pick up the distress frequency, harbour and inter-ship frequencies without you having to switch manually. This way you will not miss anything important, such as navigation warnings.

Obtain weather forecast

There should be no difficulty in getting good quality weather information. You will probably have internet access when you are in harbour but not out at sea, so get the latest information before departing. Relate what the forecast is saying to what you can see outside to get an idea of the progress of fronts and possible wind changes.

Destination marina/harbour contacted

Make a phone call to your destination harbour/marina to let them know that you are on your way.

Tide tables available

You should have the times of high and low water available so that you know what the tide is doing both in the departure harbour and along your route.

Passage plan completed

Your passage plan should be completed before departure. It can include notes on tides and VHF frequencies annotated on the charts.

Fuel checked

The fuel requirements for the proposed passage should have been calculated and checked against the fuel available.

Take time to prepare

It is easy to take many aspects of harbour navigation for granted, particularly when leaving your home harbour because you know the routine so well, but leaving from any other harbour or marina demands a degree of preparation and planning if you want things to go smoothly. You need to have planned the route for when you get outside the harbour and it can be a good idea to show this to the crew so that everybody is aware of what is going to happen. The crew can be your life-support system out at sea if things do take a turn for the worst so it makes sense to engage them in the navigation.

HARBOUR NAVIGATION

FUEL MANAGEMENT

Does the contents gauge read accurately?
It is not always easy to check the accuracy of the fuel gauge on boats unless there is a sight gauge on the tank; use a dipstick if you can. Some gauges give very vague readings so it is best to start with a full tank.

If a reserve is included, how much?
Some fuel systems incorporate a reserve that is accessed by opening a valve. Check whether the reserve is full and how much it contains.

What proportion of the tank contents can be accessed?
The fuel suction pipe rarely extends to the bottom of the tank so check how much of the contents are accessible.

Accuracy of fuel/speed figures
You should have figures that show fuel consumption against the speed of the boat. These tend to assume a clean bottom and calm seas, so err on the side of caution when using them.

Fuel per mile
The consumption figure that really matters is fuel per mile. Calculate this by dividing the consumption per hour by the speed over the ground.

How much reserve to allow?
A 20% reserve would be reasonable, i.e. 20M for every 100M you travel. Adverse weather will increase the fuel consumption.

Fuel for a secondary port
A diversion to a secondary port may increase the distance, is there enough fuel for this?

Running on one engine
If one engine is out of action and you have to run on the remaining engine the consumption per mile is likely to increase so make allowances for this possibility.

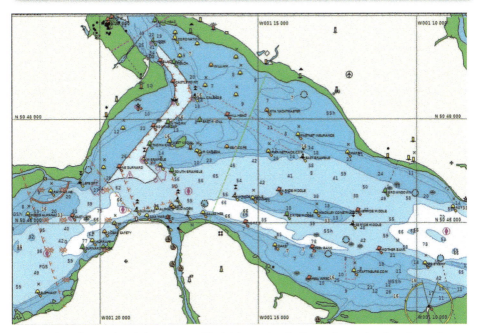

Despite the advent of GPS, buoys are still widely used to indicate the navigation channels

PRACTICAL NAVIGATION

HARBOUR NAVIGATION

Navigation checklist

It can be useful to have a navigation checklist; tick off the items to make sure that nothing gets overlooked on your way out to sea. Do remember that a checklist is only as good as the person using it and it is all too easy to tick off the boxes without actually doing the physical checks that are the important part of the system. Above is a sample navigation checklist and the steps you might take.

You can find a sudden change in conditions when passing through breakwaters

Leaving harbour

Once away from your berth or clear of the marina there are many different types of harbour you may have to navigate in:
- You may have a long and winding journey through a buoyed channel in a river or estuary
- Alternatively, just a short trip out through the harbour piers until you reach the open sea.
- There are some marinas where you clear the breakwater and are immediately out in the open sea, making a very sudden transition and facing a considerable change in the conditions.

Either way, you need to concentrate because, although going out to sea always seems to be easier than coming in, there can still be hazards.

If you are not familiar with the harbour entrance channel you are using, some preparation beforehand will be necessary because the changes can come up thick and fast. Once again, a paper chart can be a great guide to what to expect in the entrance channel but the electronic chart with its automatic plotting can also help considerably. The GPS plot of the electronic chart will normally be reasonably accurate but please don't solely rely on it; a visual check as you pass buoys and other marks is vital. At night it can be much trickier because you have to count light flashes on the buoys. It takes longer to identify each one and becomes much harder to judge distances. Leaving harbour is generally a matter of visual navigation and you need to be prepared for this. It is inadvisable to leave a

Be prepared to stop quickly when the breakwaters create a blind spot where others boats may be navigating

harbour in fog but this, and night navigation in harbours, will be covered in later chapters.

Control signals

In harbours enclosed by a breakwater you will usually have adequate water for navigation inside the breakwater but you can be blind to what is outside it. In this case there may be control signals on the breakwater that inform you whether you can leave or not. Typically, red lights mean wait and green mean proceed but check these before you leave to be sure. You will be going out of the entrance virtually blind until you clear the breakwater and won't know what is outside until you see it, so you will need to take it slow as you exit. Marinas in the Mediterranean are particularly prone to this. For marina entrances in rivers and in many enclosed harbours, be prepared to find a tide or current running across the entrance as you exit.

Checking your progress

When the harbour channel is marked by buoys it can be a good idea to tick them off

HARBOUR NAVIGATION

on the chart as you pass them so that you know where you are at all times. This can stop you heading off into the shallows when you make a turn in the harbour or if you take up your chosen course too early in the entrance. In busy commercial harbours it is sensible to keep out of the way of any ships navigating in the channel. There may be a small craft channel marked on the chart or you could check if there is adequate water just outside the line of buoys marking the main channel where you can navigate safely with your relatively shallow draught. Watching the GPS position on the electronic chart can provide a useful check on progress in harbours with a winding channel. When these are marked with buoys or beacons, you can use a combination of electronic and visual navigation, checking one against the other, to make sure you are not straying outside the channel.

Buoys

It is important to get to know the meanings of the different colours and lights of buoys. It is a bit like knowing your traffic signs on the road and in much the same way as the less common signs in the Highway Code have a tendency to fade from memory over time, you can become a bit blasé about what you're seeing on the water and make assumptions that are not justified. There's a big difference between seeing the buoys and understanding what they indicate in order to make a safe passage. Remember that buoys can be replaced by poles or beacons where the channel is fixed and these will tend to use the same colour coding.

Port and Starboard Marks

Usage Also known as lateral marks, these are the most common marks used to indicate buoys on the port or starboard side of the channel when heading into harbour or in the direction of the flood tide.

Colour Red (port) and green (starboard)

Features The shape of the buoy can give a further indication: can or square-shaped buoys mark the port side of a channel and cone or conical buoys mark the starboard side.

Lights They flash red or green in any rhythm so that each buoy can be identified by its light characteristic.

This applies to Europe but in much of the Americas the shapes of the buoys are the same but the colours are reversed.

It is an understatement to say that an understanding of buoyage is pretty important when you are heading out to sea. Even if you are an experienced mariner, it never hurts to refresh your memory so here is a brief, by no means exhaustive, overview of what buoys to look for and what they mean

You need to concentrate on the marks in a narrow channel between rocks like this

PRACTICAL NAVIGATION *37*

HARBOUR NAVIGATION

Cardinal buoy

Cardinal Marks

Usage Tend to be found offshore and are used to mark danger areas such as a shoal or rocks. You are not likely to see cardinal marks in the harbour environs but they could be found in wider estuaries.

Colour Black and yellow.

Features It is their unique topmark that indicates to which side you should pass to be in safe water. Topmarks consist of two triangles and come in four types: north, south, east and west, hence the name cardinal. Two upward pointing triangles indicate north, two down indicate south; both easy to remember. East and west are not as obvious; west topmarks point at each other and east point away. Keep to the north of a north cardinal mark and to the south of a south one etc.

Lights The lights on these buoys are not very indicative. They will be either quick flashing or very quick flashing and you will need to refer to the chart to identify an individual buoy and which side to pass it.

Fairway Buoys

Usage These are sometimes known as Sea Buoys and are used to mark the seaward end of a harbour channel. Traditionally, they are the point of departure or, when arriving, the waypoint to aim for and are used to mark the transition from open water navigation to pilotage navigation. There should be adequate water on every side of the Fairway Buoy for you to pass clear.

Colour Vertical red and white stripes

Features A ball topmark

Lights At night they can be identified by a single long white flash every 10 seconds which is designed to make them stand out from other flashing lights.

Isolated Danger Buoy

Usage These buoys are used to mark a relatively small hazard in the middle of an area of open water. They can be passed on either side although you want to give them a generous clearance because they don't normally sit directly on top of the danger except where they are beacons rather than buoys.

Colour Red with black horizontal stripes

Features Two black balls as a topmark

Lights If a light is fitted, it will be a white light flashing in groups of two.

Special Marks

Usage These buoys or marks don't have any navigational significance except to special areas or features such as yacht race turning marks, swimming or water-skiing zones, anchorages, fish farms or firing ranges etc. and whilst they do not have any navigational significance you might want to check them out, particularly if you are in an area of fish farms. Many of these marks, such as those for race courses, are seasonal.

Colour These are always yellow.

Features If there is a topmark it will be a cross

Lights If there is a light it will be yellow.

HARBOUR NAVIGATION

IALA BUOYAGE SYSTEM REGION A

Lateral marks
Port hand
All red
Topmark (if any): can
Light (if any): red

Starboard hand
All green
Topmark (if any): cone
Light (if any): green

Preferred channel to port
Green/red/green
Light (if any): Fl(2+1)G

Preferred channel to starboard
Red/green/red
Light (if any): Fl(2+1)R

Isolated danger marks
(stationed over a danger with navigable water around)
Black with red band
Topmark: 2 black balls
Light (if any): Fl(2) (white)

Special mark
Body shape optional, yellow
Topmark (if any): Yellow X
Light (if any): Fl.Y etc

Safe water marks
(mid-channel and landfall)
Red and white vertical stripes
Topmark (if any): red ball
Light (if any): Iso, Oc, LFl.10s
or Mo(A) (white)

Emergency Wreck Marking buoy
Yellow and blue vertical stripes
Topmark: upright yellow cross
Light (if any): Fl.Bu/Y.3s

Cardinal marks

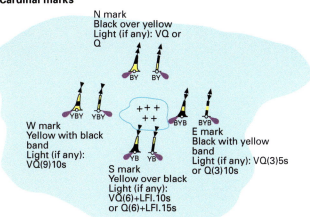

N mark
Black over yellow
Light (if any): VQ or Q

W mark
Yellow with black band
Light (if any): VQ(9)10s

E mark
Black with yellow band
Light (if any): VQ(3)5s or Q(3)10s

S mark
Yellow over black
Light (if any): VQ(6)+LFl.10s or Q(6)+LFl.15s

PRACTICAL NAVIGATION 39

HARBOUR NAVIGATION

A wooden pile as a substitute for a buoy

Lateral buoys can be placed quite close to the danger they mark

You will have gathered that buoyage can be a complicated matter and to make it worse buoys are liable to be moved at short notice if the channel changes. This is a common occurrence in harbours with a sand bar across the entrance, where the channel may change position, particularly after a storm. In larger harbours there will usually be a notice to mariners about this but smaller harbours often make changes without notice. You may also find that many of the buoys and marks in small harbours do not fully conform with the types of buoys listed above and may be very small and hard to pick out. It is likely that buoys in small harbours will not have lights on them because of the high cost of maintenance so if you are planning to visit some of these smaller harbours then a phone call to the harbour master could be a good idea to get the latest updates about navigating in that harbour.

However, buoys can give you a lot of information in addition to just marking a channel or isolated danger. They can also give you a position fix if you are passing close to them. You know where the buoy is, so you know where you are, and you don't get position fixes simpler than that. This might be more relevant to buoys in offshore waters when on passage but they can also tell you what the tidal flow is doing. It is easy to see which way the tide is flowing and to get an idea of its strength simply by seeing how the water flows around the buoy. This can be useful information particularly around the change of the tide when you may not be too sure which way the tide is flowing when you pass.

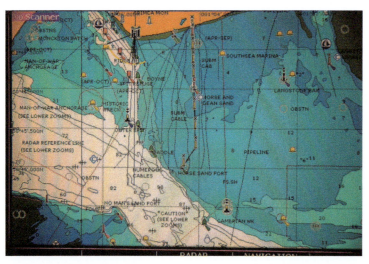

A wide variety of marks can be used to mark harbour channels

HARBOUR NAVIGATION

Lighthouse marks on the piers give a clear indication of this harbour entrance

Buoys can be laid in exposed locations and they could be missing after a storm

Entering harbour

Coming into a harbour from seaward can be much more challenging than when leaving. Firstly you have to find the entrance, which sounds easy when you have GPS as your guide but can be more difficult than you would expect. Harbour entrances are not always easy to pick out against the land, particularly if the sun is rising or setting behind the land. There may be a fairway buoy that marks the entrance and your GPS should guide you to a point close by, which will give you a reference point to work out where the channel goes from there.

When you are entering a new harbour the navigation mainly comes down to planning, working things out beforehand so that when you actually enter the harbour you have the resources to cope. You should have an idea of what you will be looking at visually and the electronic chart can provide that essential check. Looking harbours up on Google Earth before arrival can also give you a good idea of what to expect. You must be prepared for the change in navigation techniques that moving from the wide, open sea to the narrow confines of harbour can bring. These confines also apply to the depth of water under your keel and in your planning you will want to know what the tide is doing.

Conspicuous marks

Conspicuous marks can be of great use in guiding you into a harbour; look out for anything that is marked on the chart that could give you a clue. One of the advantages of the paper chart is that many conspicuous features such as tall chimneys, church spires and large buildings are marked in harbour areas because they serve as features that could be used to obtain a compass bearing.

If electronic charts are in raster format, i.e direct copies of the paper chart, you can still find these conspicuous marks, but with many vector format electronic charts many of these marks have disappeared.

Even with paper charts you need to use any labelled conspicuous features with a bit of caution because the charts do not always keep up to date with new buildings and whilst at one time there may have been just one tall building in the harbour town, several more might have been built in the meantime; a church spire might now be hidden behind new buildings along the waterfront and even chimneys get demolished. More permanent marks are likely to be lighthouses on the end of piers but even these can be hard to spot against a background of shore buildings.

Harbour entrances usually become clear once you get close

PRACTICAL NAVIGATION 41

HARBOUR NAVIGATION

Entering a breakwater harbour you cannot see what is inside until you are there

It can be challenging to pick up channel buoys when entering an estuary harbour in lively seas

Depths

Depth is another helpful tool when heading towards the land. As a general rule, the closer you get to land the shallower it gets but don't rely on this implicitly. Your harbour entrance may have a deep-water channel that has been dredged to allow big ships to enter and cliffs can sometime descend directly into quite deep water. Therefore, even with GPS leading the way, it does make sense to have the echo sounder on when approaching a harbour as an important secondary check.

Conditions

Having located your harbour entrance or fairway buoy, you might want to assess what the conditions in the entrance are likely to be, particularly if the wind is blowing in. An onshore wind combined with an ebb tide can make for nasty conditions in a harbour entrance, particularly if there is a shallow bar across it. Coming in from seaward you might not be able to clearly see the breaking waves on the bar until you are very close, so it could be a good idea to get a check on the conditions by using the radio to contact the harbour master. Even in harbours where there is a stone breakwater protecting the entrance you can find patches of rougher seas around it, created by the waves reflected back from the vertical walls of the breakwater. Both of these scenarios can come as a bit of a shock just as you think you are entering the safety of the harbour after what may have been a lively passage out at sea. When entering harbour, do not relax until you are safely mooring up.

Echo sounders

The echo sounder can be a useful guide when entering harbour but remember that it is only showing the depth directly underneath the hull and cannot give advance warning of

HARBOUR NAVIGATION

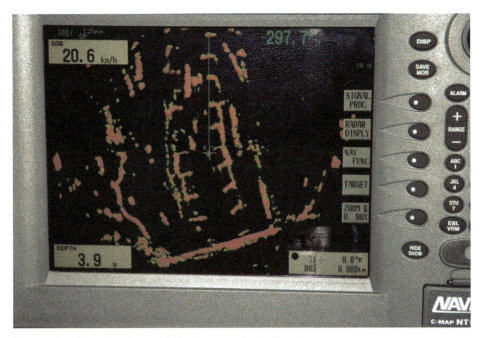

Interpreting the radar picture of a harbour can be challenging

approaching shallows. You can see the trend as the water gets deeper or shallower but at what point do you decide that you must stop because the shoaling is continuing? There is no easy answer to this and it can be nerve-racking knowing that there is a bar or a shallow spit across an entrance and watching the depth getting less and less. This is where you need to have confidence in your calculations and in the chart information, especially if you are planning to cut the margins fine.

Electronic charts

Back to the planning for entering harbour; the electronic chart can help a lot here. GPS has a reliable accuracy of possibly around 20 metres which should be enough to plot your position accurately enough all the way into harbour but there are things you need to consider before relying on GPS positioning in this way. Firstly, how accurate do you need the positioning to be in the particular harbour you are entering? In many harbours the margins can be quite tight and whilst 20 metres sounds accurate it may not be sufficient, particularly when you need to allow some margin of safety outside that 20 metre variation. Then there is the matter of the accuracy of the electronic chart that you are using to plot the position. Electronic charts do not tend to get updated at regular intervals. This can cause issues in harbours, where the channels can change over the years. The harbour authorities adapt to changes by moving buoys around so that they continue to indicate the channel but these changes may not have been added to your chart. The same issue can arise with the features along the shore in a harbour, where changes such as new piers, marina developments and jetties may occur. Electronic chart producers aim to get as much up to date information as possible but, whatever they do and however often you update your chart, it will always be out of date. Visual navigation is, therefore, key to safe navigation.

PRACTICAL NAVIGATION **43**

HARBOUR NAVIGATION

Fish farms can be a hazard in some harbour areas

GPS

GPS should be accurate enough to get you to the fairway buoy at a harbour entrance but think carefully about entering if you do not actually see the buoy. At a certain point visual navigation must take over. If you do plan to use GPS to help navigation in a harbour then try to visualise it as a circle of position in which the boat may lie. A 20 metre radius circle should be enough given the assumed accuracy of GPS but remember that in harbours you can be close to land, which is where those GPS jammers used by truckers may be operating, so be prepared for temporary GPS outages. Essentially, although GPS is a great help, harbour navigation continues to rely heavily on visual navigation and prior planning.

Harbour channel marks

Many harbour entrance channels are marked by buoys and leading lights, plus beacons and lighthouses. Each harbour will have its own combination and remember that these marks are generally laid to aid the navigation of larger ships. Often there can be plenty of water for yachts outside the main shipping channel but tread cautiously here because these areas may not be surveyed regularly. If you stick to the buoyed channel as you come in, you will be safe. Remember that if you find yourself in a fairly long stretch of buoyed channel, it is a good idea to mark off the buoys on the chart as you pass them to keep a check on where you are in the channel.

Once you pick up the buoys marking the entrance channel you should have no problem following them, provided you are entering a reasonably sized port. However, your cruising plans may be more adventurous and take you to small, out of the way ports where there is no money for buoys to mark the channel. Here, all you may find is a series of stakes or withies to mark the channel. If you plan to enter harbours like this, it pays to get some local advice before entering and often a quick phone call will confirm what you can expect to find in the entrance. Local advice can also be useful in harbours with a bar that shifts and changes with the weather. Here the buoys marking

Leading marks can give a clear indication of the channel line

Talking to the harbour authorities can give you an update on conditions inside the harbour

HARBOUR NAVIGATION

In some harbours the harbour authorities will direct you to a berth

the channel will be moved accordingly so it is useful to have up to date information on their location before entering.

Tides

There are two schools of thought regarding tides when entering harbours: there are those that maintain that entering on the flood tide is best because if you touch bottom, the rising tide will lift the boat and enable you to carry on; others say that entering on the ebb tide is better because you are stemming the tide and can easily stop and hold your position if you want to work out where to go next. It is not easy to say which side has the strongest argument; you must make the decision according to the circumstances. You do not want to be navigating by feel if you can avoid it and whilst a sailboat keel will not normally suffer damage by touching a soft bottom, the propellers may be the lowest part on a motor cruiser and so could be vulnerable if you ground. You will not want to push your luck to this sort of limit and certainly not if there are rocks around.

Don't be put off by all these cautions, most harbour entrances are straightforward and designed to make navigation easy as long as you have the right charts to show the details. Remember that you can stop and work things out if uncertainties arise on the way in, although on a strong flood tide this may be trickier.

Summary

The answer to entering a harbour successfully is to prepare thoroughly beforehand and remain alert at all times when navigating.

There are usually many clues around to help guide you in and you always have the GPS position on the electronic chart as a guide and the echo sounder as confirmation.

However, whilst it can be relatively easy to get confirmation of your position, it can be worrying if the different sources of information do not concur and you receive conflicting information. In this situation my advice would be to rely on the visual information rather than the electronic, although bear in mind that it is easy to make what you see fit into what you expected to see.

A final thing to apply caution to is the reliability of local information. If a crewmember assures you that they know the harbour well, take it with a pinch of salt and keep a careful eye on progress so you can take over if needed. After all, as the skipper, the responsibility for a safe entry is yours.

Entering a strange harbour is likely to be one of the more critical parts of navigation so stay alert to all possibilities but remember that most harbours you encounter will be well marked and designed to make navigation straightforward, enabling you should be able to enter without any problems.

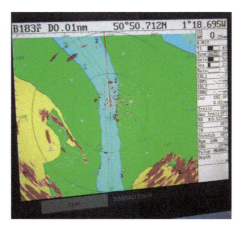

The radar overlay may not always correspond directly with the electronic chart display in narrow channels

5 Coastal navigation

Isolated lighthouses can be a distinctive feature when navigating

Once you leave harbour, most of your navigation is likely to be along a coastline but you may also find yourself heading across the seas to foreign lands. Both navigational scenarios will be covered in this chapter but we will start by looking at how to navigate along a coastline when, in normal visibility, you should have the land in sight the majority of the time.

Distinctive features

With the land in sight you will have lots of visual clues about your position.

- Hills, cliffs and coastal towns onshore can give you some idea of your progress.
- Lighthouses are only likely to be found on headlands although there are exceptions, such as Eddystone and Wolf Rock lighthouses, which mark isolated rocks in the open sea.
- Buoys may mark shoals in shallower areas, such as the North Sea.

The GPS will, of course, plot your progress along your chosen route to the next waypoint but, as ever, visual checks are a good back up to confirm that all is well.

This TV mast is an easy to identify, distinctive feature and has red lights at night

Comparing what you see outside with what the paper chart shows

46 PRACTICAL NAVIGATION

COASTAL NAVIGATION

The twin chimneys and the large white building are distinctive features and, combined with the buoy, provide vital navigation clues

Certain light conditions can make it difficult to pick out features and marks

Planning your route

Buoys and marks

It can be useful to plan a route that passes close to isolated buoys, beacons and lighthouses. If you are planning a voyage across the English Channel, for example, there are buoys marking the big ship channels and one-way systems and sighting these can provide useful reassurance that you are on track. Some of these offshore and isolated marks will also be fitted with a Racon beacon, designed to make them easy to identify on the radar and to make them stand out from any other targets nearby. You may find similar Racon beacons on major fairway buoys, which can be useful if the visibility is restricted.

Depths

The echo sounder can provide another means of checking your position. Looking at the chart it can often be possible to identify shoal areas with plenty of water for you to pass over them; these will show up on the sounder trace and provide you with a check on your position. Where the water shoals gradually there will not be a clear-cut position indication but any shoal that has a steep-to edge will provide a clear position line. The same can be achieved in areas of deeper water depths such as Hurd Deep in the English Channel. Practising this visual, radar or echo sounder checking will not only add interest to the voyage but will

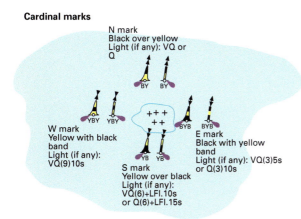

Cardinal marks

N mark
Black over yellow
Light (if any): VQ or Q

W mark
Yellow with black band
Light (if any): VQ(9)10s

S mark
Yellow over black
Light (if any): VQ(6)+LFl.10s or Q(6)+LFl.15s

E mark
Black with yellow band
Light (if any): VQ(3)5s or Q(3)10s

PRACTICAL NAVIGATION **47**

COASTAL NAVIGATION

A navigation buoy marking a shoal extending offshore from the headland

make it much easier for you to cope should the GPS positioning let you down for any reason.

Waypoints

You will almost certainly have plotted a route on a chart plotter, which means that it will be identified by a series of waypoints. A waypoint is a latitude and longitude marking the spot where you will need to alter course; it will often be found at a point that is physically marked at or close to a buoy. As such, the same point may be used by a number of other boats on passage, leading to congestion around some of these turning marks on a fine summer's day. It may, therefore, be better to select a point a little distance away from the buoy so that you don't get caught in the crowds but are still close enough to see the mark. It is a relatively easy job to move a waypoint on an electronic system, typically by dragging it to the new position or 'rubber banding' the course to create a new waypoint along an established course line.

Autopilot

There is no doubt that GPS positioning will be your prime method of navigation in coastal waters but you have options regarding how you use it. These relate to the use of autopilot control. The link between chart plotter and autopilot means that you can instruct the autopilot to follow the route plotted on the chart all the way from

Comparing the visual sighting with what is shown on the paper chart

48 PRACTICAL NAVIGATION

departure to arrival. The autopilot will alter course automatically when you reach a waypoint and keep the boat on track, correcting for any deviations from the chosen route. This method of cruising could be adopted by a motor cruiser but with a sailboat, where wind direction must be taken into account, this level of automation is not likely to work well as it will not cope with any temporary changes in wind direction caused by gusts.

Even for a motor cruiser this level of automation is not recommended. Do you really want the autopilot to make a major alteration of course automatically at a waypoint without any allowance for any other craft that may be around you? I simply cannot imagine navigating with this level of automation; sitting back to relax whilst the electronics take over. If nothing else, Colregs require you to keep a good lookout at all times. You might choose to set up the autopilot to keep the boat on the chosen track between waypoints, without altering course on arrival at them. With this set up, the system will make small alterations to the course to keep the boat on track and compensate for the tide and winds, but even here it is better for you to make these corrections manually in order to be aware of what is going on the whole time. The autopilot is a wonderful tool and can relieve you of the monotony of manual steering and allow you concentrate on the look out and boat management, but it must be used intelligently.

Manual steering

On a sailboat, and possibly even on a motor cruiser, you might wish to maintain manual steering. On a sailboat this could be because you want to optimise the course to keep the sails working effectively and enable you to cope with the small changes in wind direction and speed that will constantly occur, particularly when sailing along a coastline. You will have the compass as your steering reference for this but how accurate is your compass? It is rare to find a magnetic compass that has been fully corrected to take out the errors and even then you still have to

apply the variation in order to find a true course that you can reference to the chart. This is where your chart plotter and the GPS can be very helpful. You will steer the course as best you can but most people when steering by compass not only allow the boats's heading to wander 5° or more off course but they will tend to bias the course so that the average course steered is likely to be a few degrees to one side or the other of the chosen course that you planned. Before GPS, steering an accurate course was essential for navigation because you worked out your position by plotting the estimated course and speed. Nowadays, with the chart plotter, you can gain an immediate indication of whether the boat has been set to one side or other of the chosen track by either looking at the plot or reading the cross track error box. It is then a simple matter to bring the boat back on track by an adjustment of the course being steered.

Compasses

Compasses are changing and, whilst the basic magnetic compass is still necessary as the one navigational instrument that does not require any power supply, there are a variety of electronic units available. There is more detail on this in Chapter 11. Steering by compass is never easy and requires a degree of concentration that can distract you from other navigational requirements. It can be even more difficult maintaining a course in lively seas, when the compass may be swinging around a bit and you have to average out the readings. When you are navigating along a coastline it can be much easier to maintain your course visually, with reference to a headland or some other mark or feature ahead, a quick glance telling you whether you are on course or not. There will often be a convenient headland ahead to use as a steering reference and even though it may be slightly to one side of your chosen heading it will still work. Indeed, along many coastlines you can simply steer from one headland to the next, allowing, of course, for the need to pass a safe distance off the headland and for any tides or wind set that may set you in or out from it.

COASTAL NAVIGATION

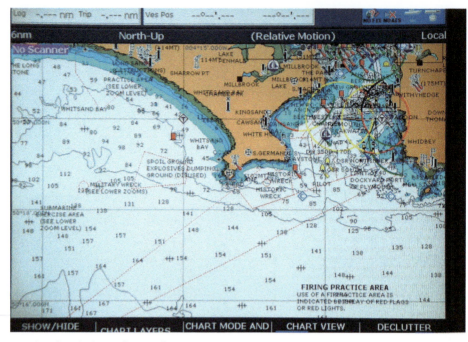

Pressing the 'declutter' button (bottom right) would help to clarify this complex chart picture

Steering references

You can apply the same principle to electronic systems, and can line up the course to be steered with direct reference to a headland. With the radar it is quite easy to estimate the distance you want to pass off the headland and then set the heading maker to that distance by adjusting the course being steered. The range rings on the radar can be used as an aid to estimating the distance that you will pass off the headland ahead. With the chart plotter you need a bit more care when setting up a passing distance off a headland in this way. You will have your chosen route marked on the screen and may then find that there are two heading markers shown (these two heading references are usually displayed in different colours):

- One of these will be the actual course being made good over the ground, which can differ from the plotted route. The average heading over the ground should remain reasonably static.
- The other is the actual heading of the boat at that particular time, calculated from successive GPS positions. The actual heading marker will move around as the heading changes.

You can usually switch one or both of these heading markers off if you wish but it is quite easy to set up a course to steer by watching the actual real time heading marker in reference to its distance off the headland and noting the course at that time. With the chart plotter heading reference there is always a short delay before the heading marker shows the actual heading, as this has to be calculated from the satellite positions of a few seconds ago. Using this type of steering reference keeps you in touch

Approaching your destination, the navigation features will gradually be revealed

COASTAL NAVIGATION

with the actual navigation situation and relates what is happening outside with what the GPS positioning is saying, giving you a much better awareness of what is going on.

Coastlines with bays

A coastline with significant bays along it provides you with options for setting the route, potentially enabling you to make better progress and, in adverse conditions, to improve the conditions on board. In a sailboat you cannot make progress directly into the wind and for a significant angle on each side of the wind direction. This can mean you must head out to sea or into the bay to allow close-hauled sailing. In a motor cruiser, life on board can also be quite uncomfortable if you head directly into the wind and sea and you can get an improved ride with reduced pitching if you put the wind at an angle on the bow, which effectively increases the wavelength. In both cases you have the option of either heading out to sea to find stronger tides to speed you on your way, or heading into a bay.

There can be considerable attractions in heading into a bay rather than taking the direct route between headlands:

- it will add surprisingly little extra to the distance and you may even make better progress.

- heading into the bay will put the wind on the bow, which on a sailboat should allow good sailing and on a motor cruiser, a more comfortable ride.

- by heading into the bay you will eventually move under the shelter of the land as you approach the next headland which should allow you to make better and more comfortable progress thanks to the reduced sea conditions.

- if the tide is with you, you may lose some of its strength when heading into the bay

The complex tidal streams around Portland Bill, which can be challenging for low powered yachts

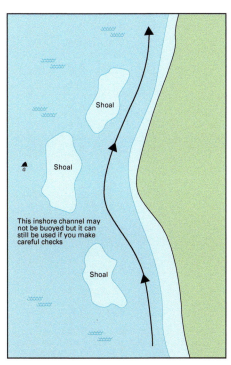

Unmarked inshore channels may be a viable alternative but you will need to concentrate and keep the sounder running if you use one. Always be ready to stop if you don't like what you see

- but this should be balanced out by the increased tide as the water gets squeezed up on the approach to the headland.
- even in fine conditions there are advantages in heading into a bay rather than taking the direct route; the closer to the land you are, the more interesting the scenery and the better you will be able to keep a check on progress.

Keep your echo sounder running as you head into the bay to ensure that you do not run into shallow water and check the chart for any displayed dangers before you head inshore.

Headland conditions

Rounding a headland can be an interesting navigational experience and you need to study the particular headland and its adjacent waters before taking it on. There are many different types of headland:

- those with high cliffs that drop cleanly into relatively deep water
- those with offshore rocks stretching out to sea
- those low-lying with shoals in the waters offshore or adjacent to the side of the headland
- others where there can be quite a tide race as the tidal flow increases around the headland.

Tidal flows and races

A unique feature of some headlands where there is a strong tidal flow and a tide race is a relatively smooth patch of water close in off the headland and inside the main tide race. This can be used as a means of rounding the headland close-to rather than going a considerable way offshore to avoid the breaking seas of the tide race. Portland Bill and the Mull of Kintyre are like this and at Portland you need to be as close as 200–300 metres off the headland to get the benefit of the calmer waters inshore. Here you can also experience a tide race at the side of the headland where the tidal flow spins around after passing the headland and encounters the main tidal flow causing a confused sea.

The tidal flow can run up to around 5 knots in some of these areas off headlands and you might hesitate to use the inshore channel in a sailboat or a low powered motor cruiser. You are reducing the safety margins using these inshore channels and need to make a decision about the risks

You need special equipment to pick up weather chart information at sea but it can be vital for ocean cruising

involved if you lose power or the wind drops. In your passage planning you will have aimed to pass any significant headlands when the tide is flowing with your direction of travel to get maximum benefit but on a longer passage you probably will not be able to get a favourable tide at each headland so will have to be selective.

Wind around headlands

The wind will also increase around a headland, particularly those with high cliffs. Alternatively, you may experience patches of lighter winds. In the Mediterranean you will not have tidal streams but you can find a significant increase in wind strength and, hence, deterioration in sea conditions in some areas. The Strait of Bonifacio, where the wind flows between the high cliffs of Corsica and Sardinia, is noted for this and you can experience the same conditions in the Strait of Messina between Italy and Sicily. In tidal waters any wind-against-tide situation will cause the waves to become steeper and more difficult to negotiate, particularly in a tidal race, so you need to plan for this and, where possible, keep well offshore, where any effect may be less severe.

Rocks and shoals

Where rocks or shoals extend out from a headland without an inshore passage there is only one course to be taken. Heading into a bay when navigating along a coast of this type may not be viable. Where a shoal extends for some way offshore waves may break over the shoal due to the restricted tidal flow, which then accelerates as it lifts over the shoal; areas where this occurs are best avoided. These areas can be found even in light winds and you can usually get more information about them and tide races off headlands by studying the chart or from information in pilot guides. However, you will have to make you own assessment of them based on the prevailing conditions of wind and tide.

Navigation along a coast is not, therefore, a simple case of plotting a safe route on the electronic chart and then following it. You need to take the wind and sea conditions

> ## HOURLY CHECKS ON PASSAGE
>
> ### Fill in log book
> This can seem an unnecessary chore but having a record of courses and positions is valuable if you have an electrical or electronic failure. You can also see weather trends.
>
> ### Engine compartment
> A regular check in the engine compartment can enable you to detect any leaks or problems before they get serious.
>
> ### Weather forecast
> Update the weather forecast at regular intervals if you can.
>
> ### Course and position
> Check both the course you are steering and the course being followed on the plotter and adjust if necessary.
>
> ### Double checking
> Try to check the position by visual means or with the echo sounder if you are within sight of land to confirm that the GPS is working satisfactorily.
>
> ### Fuel
> If you are running under power, check the fuel being used and the fuel remaining to ensure that you are not consuming more than expected.
>
> ### Crew
> Check that the crew are all OK and in good shape. Look for any signs of seasickness.

into account and make your own assessment of what is viable, using up-to-date information. Electronic chart systems featuring tidal flow charts and wind information can be valuable in helping you to make your assessment. However, although the tidal information is likely to be quite accurate, the wind and sea information is much more general and will not take into account any local conditions where the wind strength increases around a headland or in narrow channels. The forecast wind strength will not include the gusts, which can double

COASTAL NAVIGATION

the wind strength temporarily and the forecast of wave heights can be similarly approximate. Wave height is very variable with, on average, one wave in 22 being twice the average height, even in consistent wind conditions, and the very occasional random wave reaching as much as four times the average height. Averages do not count for much when you experience one of these rogue waves but they are more likely to be found with very strong winds when you should be safely tucked up in harbour.

Navigating in open seas

Heading across open seas, away from the coast, takes you away from any coastal dangers but brings its own considerations. The tide will often be on your beam, setting you to one side or the other of your course line and you will need to compensate for this. You can build in a course correction of a few degrees to compensate at the start of the crossing, bearing in mind, of course, that the faster your boat the less correction you will need. Alternatively, you may wish to add

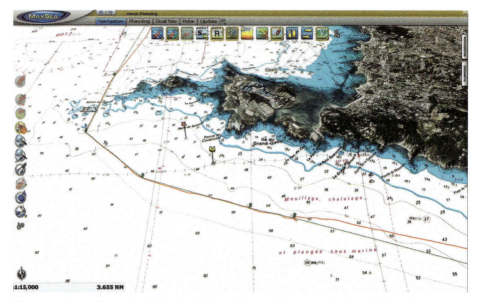

The green shows the route plotted and the red shows the course that was followed

The first sighting of distant land can be an exciting time

54 PRACTICAL NAVIGATION

COASTAL NAVIGATION

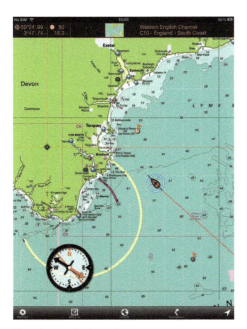

The electronic chart shows you are approaching land; this is the time when you should make your first sighting

corrections to the course during the voyage, as and when you notice the cross track error increasing. There are also specialised computer applications that can process the corrections for you as you go along. These are usually software-based programmes that can be used on a laptop or PC and we will look at them in more detail in the computer chapter. No corrections may be needed at all if you anticipate a 12-hour crossing, as the tide one way should cancel out the tide in the other direction.

Making a landfall

At the end of one of a crossing you will have to make a landfall. This is always an exciting moment when navigating and with GPS positioning it should be a fairly straightforward exercise but try to choose a landfall position where there is some readily identifiable object on the land so as to have confirmation of the landfall position when it is sighted. A lighthouse makes a particularly suitable landmark as you will be able to identify it by day or night but other

MAKING A LANDFALL

Selecting the landfall point
The landfall is the critical part of any voyage, so try to select a landfall point that is easily recognisable. Even with modern electronics it is good to have a visual check.

Using the depth sounder
The depth sounder can give you an additional position check as you close the land and give early warning of any dangers.

Conspicuous objects
There are often conspicuous objects marked on the chart and these can be very useful as a reference point to locate a harbour entrance.

Off-lying dangers
There may be off-lying dangers around your landfall point so check the chart carefully, on a large scale, to identify these and make sure you pass clear.

Angle of approach
If you approach the land at a shallow angle rather than at right angles, it is easier to turn away should you detect any unexpected dangers or problems.

Shore lights
Be aware that at night it can be challenging to identify flashing lights and the lights on other vessels against the background of shore lights.

GPS
The accurate positions given by the GPS can give you a lot of confidence when making your approach but, as ever, try to confirm your position by other means as well.

possibilities could be a distinctive headland or hill or a feature such as a wind farm or oil platform/drilling rig. Have the sounder on when making a landfall and if you have radar you will often be able to identify high land on the radar before you sight it visually. Before GPS it was wise to offset the position

COASTAL NAVIGATION

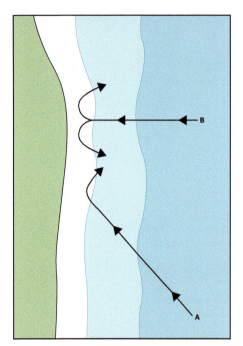
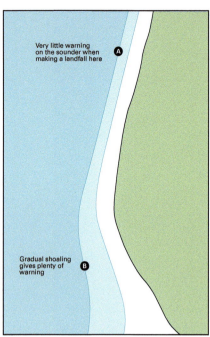

When making a landfall in poor visibility it is better to approach at the angle shown in A. Approaching directed (as in B) means having to turn through a greater angle if sudden shoaling is detected and you will be unsure which is the safefest way to turn

When the beach is steep-to there will be little warning of the approach as at A.
Landfall at B will give more warning and allow time to take action

of your landfall to one side or the other of the actual required landfall position so that when you sighted the land you would know which way to turn to find your destination. There may be less need for this today thanks to the accurate position fixing of GPS but it does no harm to do it, just in case the GPS lets you down.

Alarms

There are a number of alarms incorporated into electronic systems on board that can be set as a further check that everything is going according to plan and to warn of any aberrations. The autopilot failure alarm should warn you of any failure in the system such as a loss of power, a compass input sensor failure or if the course steered moves a certain amount from the preset course to steer. The chart plotter, meanwhile, may have several alarms, some of which can be pre-set. The most obvious one indicates a loss of the GPS signal; this alarm may be repeated by some of the other electronic systems on board, such as the AIS and the radar. Amongst the other alarms that you can set is one to identify an increase in the cross track error and warn of a deviation from the preset course above a certain distance. You can also set a proximity alarm for approaching land or waypoints and, on some more sophisticated systems, there is a depth alarm, which warns you when you are entering shallow water according to the charted depths.

Radar also offers a proximity alarm, indicating when a target is approaching within the pre-set distance. Here the target could be land or another vessel, the first being useful for navigation and the second for collision avoidance. Finally, there are alarms that can be set on the sounder to warn of the water depth reaching a preset low level.

COASTAL NAVIGATION

Setting the aforementioned alarms for safe navigation can provide a useful warning in the event of any deviations from the planned route or of any system failure. However, you should, of course, be monitoring all these factors anyway if you are on watch and alert to what is going on. The alarms are not a substitute for keeping a lookout and monitoring the navigation situation and should not be overly relied upon.

With the potential to set so many alarms, many of which monitor a single situation, you could find yourself with several going off simultaneously. Dealing with a cacophony of alarms or flashing screen indicators can easily take your attention away from the actual navigation. This was clearly evidenced by the investigation into a GPS failure on a ship that showed that 18 separate alarms were set off by the failure. These alarms so diverted the attention of the officer on watch that the ship had been aground for 10 minutes before he realised it! The moral here is to first learn what the various alarms mean and to then understand how to deal with them if they go off. It is easy to put blind faith in the warnings and alarms to keep you out of danger but there is no excuse for not keeping a close watch on what is going on; the navigation situation must be monitored at all times.

Offshore structures

In the past, there was more or less complete freedom over where you could navigate at sea, with the exception of one or two areas reserved for military activities. These days, coastal waters can be a lot more restricted by offshore oil structures, wind, wave and tidal generating systems, and fish farms. If you keep your charts up to date all of these should be marked and it should be apparent that some of these facilities have exclusion zones around them. For instance, offshore oil platforms, both fixed and temporary, have an exclusion zone of 500 metres. During the construction of wind farms there is usually an exclusion zone in place in the area, this can cover a considerable area of several square miles. When the wind farm is established, there is a 50 metre exclusion zone around each pylon. This should not worry you too much as most of these offshore wind farms are built in shoal water areas. Sailboats should, however, bear in mind that there could be considerable wind disturbance in the lee of a pylon so it is best to give them a wide berth anyway.

Tidal and wave energy systems can be installed in various channels and open sea areas but they are generally located away from main cruising areas. Only the more adventurous cruiser should need to consider these and they should be marked with lights and buoys. Wave energy systems, which mainly float on the surface, can be a particular hazard to navigation and notices to mariners should promulgate details of new ones. Both types of renewable energy generating systems are still in their infancy but they are likely to expand as the technology becomes established and may present a considerable hazard to navigation in the future. Fish farms are now well established and tend to be found in remote, sheltered waters such as the Scottish lochs. Again, the more adventurous sailor is most likely to be concerned by them. The hazards are marked in various ways, both by day and by night, and the Marine Guidance note MGN 372 (M+F) issued by the MCA (available online) will give you most of the details.

Chart updates

It would be pleasing to think that all of these dangers to navigation would be marked on the charts but neither paper nor electronic charts can ever be fully up-to-date. It can be quite expensive to keep electronic chart cartridges up-to-date and with most of them you have to purchase an annual subscription for updates.

Admiralty charts

www.ukho.gov.uk

Updates for paper charts can be found online using the Admiralty Notices to Mariners (ANM), which is issued on a weekly basis but it can be a laborious to add these to your chart. They are numbered for the charts in

COASTAL NAVIGATION

Fish farms can be a hazard but tend to be located in more sheltered waters

the Admiralty chart range, but it can take time to add them to other charts and the stick-on patches showing changes can only be applied to the Admiralty charts.

Imray charts

www.imray.com

Imray, the other main source of paper charts for yachts and small craft, uploads weekly chart corrections to its website, where you will find all the latest changes listed in a relatively easy format.

It is a good idea to check any applicable changes before you start a cruise and either make a note of them or pencil in areas of change on the paper chart.

Electronic charts

There is no way of adding updated information to electronic chart cartridges other than by using the vague mark notation possibilities contained within the system and here you might want to add one of the signs that you can use to mark fishing locations or similar that will act as a reminder.

This will at least take away some of the surprise of seeing unexplained lights at night or coming across a buoy that is not shown on the chart and wondering what it marks. You may also come across temporary moored structures or working vessels out at sea that are, perhaps, carrying out exploratory drilling operations or pipe-laying; give these a wide berth because they may have moorings laid out some considerable distance from the structure or vessel.

A combination of buoys and lighthouses can be enough for visual navigation

COASTAL NAVIGATION

Other sources of updates

VHF You may hear about temporary obstacles to navigation via VHF radio broadcasts but there is no guarantee of this.

Navtex Information can also be found on Navtex but you should always prepare for the unexpected in coastal waters and even further offshore.

Local Notices to Mariners When entering harbours you may find that there are local Notices to Mariners about both permanent and temporary changes but these are unlikely to be broadcast over the harbour radio except, perhaps, if there is dredging taking place in the channels. The harbour's website can be a useful source of reference for changes in the local area.

Summary

Coastal navigation used to be fairly straightforward and the main requirement was to keep away from shoal and rocks. However, coastal waters are becoming increasingly crowded and the harvesting of energy, either in the form of renewables or in the form of oil and gas, has complicated coastal navigation.

It is increasingly common to encounter the unexpected, so a good lookout and concentration are needed for a safe passage but this is, of course, what you should be doing when out at sea anyway, whether obstructions are anticipated or not.

Traffic Separation Scheme (TSS)

Another situation in which you may find your route restricted is when navigating in a Traffic Separation Scheme (TSS) area.

These areas are marked on charts in the now familiar purple colour and you will need to know where and how you can navigate in them. If you are actually using the marked separation channels, you must only use them in the direction indicated. If you have a vessel that is over 20 metres in length, you are obliged to use these main marked channels unless you are heading for a port along the coast in the vicinity. You don't want to be in the main channels and the big ships do not want you there but you are not offered a choice by the rules and there can be hefty fines for not complying.

The inshore zones are there to provide a safer option for smaller craft (or indeed sailing vessels of any size, and fishing vessels provided they are fishing) and they can often provide a shorter, and certainly safer, route when navigating along a coast.

If you aim to cross the main shipping channels to get from one side to the other, as you might in the Dover Strait, you must do so at right angles to the main flow of the channel. This means that it is the course you steer that must be at right angles to the main channel, rather than the course made good.

Use of the separation zone between the main channels is not permitted except when crossing or in emergencies. **If you are less than 20 metres in length or a sailing vessel, you are not allowed to impede the passage of ships using the main shipping lanes. You must, therefore, give way to them at all times.** If you cannot make progress under sail in the traffic lane because of the wind direction then you must use your engine and become a power driven vessel.

The rules are complicated but if you plan to navigate in the regions where the TSS exist then you need to understand them in detail in order to conform. The best solution is to avoid the big ships if your size and the rules allow it and, in most cases, this is possible if you plan ahead.

You also need to take extra care at the beginning and end of any separation zone, where ships could be heading off or arriving from a variety of directions.

PRACTICAL NAVIGATION

6 Collision avoidance

So far we have dealt with navigation in terms of finding your way. An equally important topic to consider is collision avoidance. The principal difference between the two is that routes can be planned in advance whereas collision avoidance must, for the most part, be dealt with as and when situations occur.

You can plan a route that should help to keep you away from encounters with big ships, keeping out of the main shipping lanes and, when close to the coast, keeping in shallower waters where the big ships cannot go.

You can also make sure that your boat is as visible as possible to other craft, so that they are aware of your presence, but most of the time your actions will be dictated by the movements of other vessels that you encounter along the way and the action that they may or may not take.

It is a little like two pedestrians meeting on a pavement, both taking avoidance action at the same time which may or may not end in collision, but at sea there is a strict set of rules that dictate the action that each vessel should take to avoid close encounters of the wrong kind. This would make collision avoidance a simple matter if only all vessels stuck to the rules.

COLREGS

The International Regulations for the Prevention of Collisions at Sea (Colregs) is a set of rules that has been developed over many years in order to comprehensively cover most scenarios that are likely to occur in ship and boat encounters at sea. As the skipper of a boat, you must have a thorough understanding of all elements of the regulations. They clearly define the responsibility that you undertake when you set sail, with Rule 2 stating

> 'Nothing in these rules shall exonerate the owner, master or crew from the consequences of any neglect to comply with these rules or the neglect of any precaution which may be required by the ordinary practice of seamen or by the special circumstances of the case.'

In other words, you can't blame the rules if you have a collision and commonsense and seamanship must prevail. The rules go on to describe what is meant by a variety of terms such as a sailing vessel and hovercraft and it is important to note that even wind surfers and jet ski drivers must conform to the rules.

The Colregs have been very carefully developed so as to leave very few exclusions or 'get out clauses'; there is to be no deviation from the rules except for the use of seamanship and commonsense where, for example, you might allow a big ship the right of way rather than expecting it to conform and give way to you.

You should not need a reminder like this at the helm

Yachts and large ships are not a healthy mix in narrow channels

COLLISION AVOIDANCE

In narrow channels you keep to starboard but try to give shipping priority

The rules are divided into several sections:
Any visibility The section that starts at Rule 4 applies in any condition of visibility
Restricted visibility A further section of rules apply in restricted visibility
In proximity of other vessels A third section is for application when vessels are in sight of one another.

You need to make yourself aware of the full meaning and application of the rules as part of your duty as a skipper. It would require another book to look at all the fine detail but there are some features that are worth explaining.

Maintain a visual lookout

Under Rule 5 you are required to maintain a proper lookout by sight and hearing as well as by all other available means appropriate to the prevailing conditions. This means that by law you cannot solely rely on electronic systems, particularly radar, to maintain a lookout; you must uphold a visual lookout all the time.

Always consider the three-screen situation when navigating:

- the electronic chart screen
- the radar screen
- the windscreen.

You may not have a radar on board, in which case the visual lookout is your only way of monitoring what is going on around you apart, perhaps, from the use of AIS. However, AIS is not mandatory on small craft so you cannot rely on that for collision avoidance. Electronic chart systems do a great job in telling you where you are and where you are going but do not keep you in contact with the transient targets that are other vessels unless they incorporate radar or AIS overlays.

On a sailboat you tend to have good visibility all around the horizon, provided that the sails do not block the view. However, do take the trouble to look astern occasionally as faster boats can creep up on you quite quickly without you being aware of them. An overtaking boat is required to keep out of your way but you are under an obligation to maintain your course and speed if being overtaken; be careful not to tack across its bows and always check astern before making any course change. Be aware, also, that a low-cut jib could create a considerable blind spot at the bow; you will need to look around or under it at frequent intervals.

Under the Colregs there is no defence for not seeing another vessel, even if that other vessel is required to give way to you.

On a motor boat your view of the outside world can be much more restricted, both by wide window mullions that support the wheelhouse windows and by a limited or completely blocked view astern. I have seen motor cruiser wheelhouses where these mullions can be over a foot wide, big enough to hide a supertanker behind, so unless you

COLLISION AVOIDANCE

That distant vessel needs careful watching as it gets closer

Visibility can be quite limited from the inside helm of some motor boats

move about and peer round the corners of the windscreen you could easily miss a smaller boat coming close. Often on a motor cruiser there is no view astern from the helm, so, whatever the speed of your boat, you must check astern at frequent intervals and ALWAYS check before making any course alteration. Even if your boat is quite fast, it is arrogant to assume that you are the fastest boat out there and that nothing will come up behind. If you really want to know what is going on around you then you should use the flybridge helm, unless you are in the open cockpit of a sports boat.

Listen for signals

The rules require you to keep a lookout by ear as well as by eye, this again suggests that you should be at an open helm station. You might think that nobody uses fog signals these days and it has, certainly, been a long time since I heard one but the requirement to use it is there and will again require an open helm if you are to fulfil it. Remember that the Colregs have been developed to leave no room for negotiation.

Refer to radar

The 'all available means' required for keeping a lookout under the Colregs also refer to radar use. If you have a working radar on board, you are required to have it switched on whatever the state of visibility and to check it for vessel targets in the same way that you would with a visual lookout. The radar and the visual lookout are complimentary and one does not replace the other. Checking the radar could be a challenge on a sailboat where the display may be located down below, at the chart table. In addition to having the radar on you must also use it to make a full appraisal of the situation and the risk of collision. With both visual and radar lookouts, appraisal of the situation usually means taking a bearing of an approaching target to assess whether a risk of collision exists. If the bearing does not change appreciably, there is a risk of collision and you must either take avoidance action or stand on as required by the rules.

Take avoidance action

Although the rules appear to cover all scenarios, you still need to make certain assumptions. Vessels are placed into two categories:

- the stand on vessel
- the vessel that must take the avoidance action.

Passing clear across the bows so you can relax a little

62 PRACTICAL NAVIGATION

COLLISION AVOIDANCE

This is intended to help avoid a scenario where both try to give way and end up by colliding. However, you must never assume that the other vessel has seen you or that it will take action to avoid collision even if it is the give way vessel.

There is nothing in the rules that states that, as the stand on vessel, you can keep going irrespective of the other boat's actions; this would put you both into danger. Once again commonsense and seamanship must prevail.

One solution is to take early avoidance action, making any such action a significant alteration of course, clearly visible to the other vessel.

A reduction in speed can also be a viable option, although one that will be less immediately obvious to the other vessel.

Limitations of radar

Radar can be a very important tool for collision avoidance but you need to understand what it can and cannot do. Small boat radars come in many forms and in order to see the detail on the display you need the largest screen that you can afford.

Big ship targets will stand out clearly and not be difficult to detect but the returns from small craft are much weaker so a quality radar system is important. The returns from targets are usually heavily processed before they are displayed; this helps to discriminate between spurious and real targets and to make the weak returns from small craft stand out on the display.

Some modern radars offer a split screen display with one section on a range of, for example, 6M to give early warning of approaching targets and the other on, say, 3M which you use for the actual collision avoidance tactics.

Even so, if you are going to use radar for collision avoidance, you need more than a quick glance to pick out small targets and determine what they are. The view from the wheelhouse window or cockpit remains the best and cheapest system for collision avoidance when conditions allow.

Overtaking in narrow channels puts the onus on you to keep clear

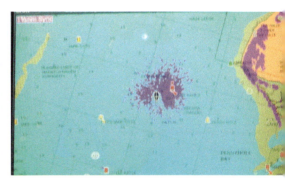

Rain showers can severely handicap the radar detection but this chart overlay shows the buoy clearly

> The trend for ships to focus on electronic rather than visual information is demonstrated by the story of one officer on watch who informed his Captain, as he joined him on the bridge
>
> 'There's a target on the radar, two miles ahead.'
>
> The Captain replied
> 'Yes, it's a yacht'.
>
> 'How do you know that it's a yacht?' asked the officer.
>
> The captain responded
> 'Because I can see it out of the window!'
>
> This demonstrates the importance of keeping a lookout by all possible means, especially the view from the window, in order to have full awareness of what is happening around you.

PRACTICAL NAVIGATION

COLLISION AVOIDANCE

Using AIS to keep a lookout

A further means of keeping a lookout is provided by the Automatic Identification System (AIS). AIS is a system where the course, speed and position of a vessel, as well as other relevant information, is transmitted automatically over a VHF link.

There are various ways in which this information can be received and presented on board. The AIS may be incorporated into your VHF radio, with the information on other vessels displayed on a built-in small screen. This gives a very basic display of vessels around you, with a vector line indicating the relative course and speed of other vessels.

This VHF has an AIS display but it is too small for practical purposes except to indicate possible dangers

You can also get AIS units that are receive-only and do not send out a signal to other vessels with information about who you are and what you are doing.

Another system allows the vectors of other vessels to be displayed on the radar or electronic chart display or both. This has to be the preferred option as it allows targets on the radar to be directly recognised on a much better scale than with the very small displays used on most dedicated units.

Like all electronic systems, you need to understand a bit more about AIS and how it works before you can use it well. Whilst the receive-only AIS units will give you information about vessels around you, these vessels will not be able to see you on their displays, making a collision much more likely.

AIS is not compulsory for vessels except those over 300 tons gross tonnage. This means that ships have AIS installed but many small craft do not and there is a now a growing trend for ships to assume that there is nothing out there except for ships and boats that show up on an AIS display.

AIS targets on a radar display with a warning that one is a potential danger

64 PRACTICAL NAVIGATION

COLLISION AVOIDANCE

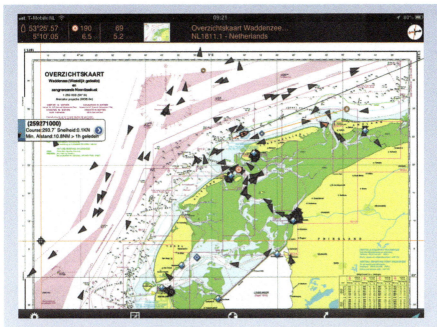

AIS targets plotted off the Dutch coast indicate the density of shipping traffic

If you don't have it or if it is not working, you may not exist on their radar screens and with ships often keeping their 'lookout' solely by radar, contrary to the rules, the weak radar return from small craft could be overlooked if there is no AIS link. You may find yourself similarly focussed on targets that are linked to AIS on your radar because they are clear and distinct but you must take care not to ignore the tiny small vessel targets from non-AIS fitted vessels.

It is very much a case of electronic developments taking two steps forward and one step backwards as the hidden consequences of this new system are revealed. AIS is a great asset for collision avoidance but be fully aware of its limitations and learn and understand just what it can and cannot do.

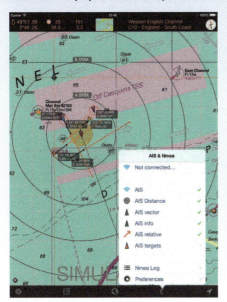

AIS targets can make the radar/chart picture more complicated and vessels without AIS could easily get missed

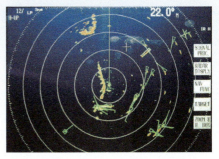

In busy waters the AIS displays can take you away from the vital visual lookout

PRACTICAL NAVIGATION

COLLISION AVOIDANCE

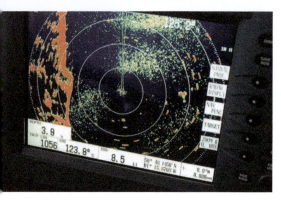

Rain can severely limit the radar detection but AIS targets will still show up

Risk of collision

When you have a target visible, either on the radar or by sight, you need to determine if it presents a collision risk. The Colregs are quite specific here.

'Every vessel shall use all available means appropriate to the prevailing circumstances and conditions to determine if risk of collision exists. If there is any doubt then such risk shall be deemed to exist.'

Again they tell you how to do this.

'Such risk shall be deemed to exist if the compass bearing of an approaching vessel does not appreciably change.'

Take the target's bearing

You must, therefore, take the target's bearing to check whether it is changing. However, very few small boats are now fitted with a compass that allows you to take a bearing, although you could use a hand-bearing compass if you have one on board.

There is an alternative method but for it to work you need to be maintaining a steady course. Stand in one place and line up the target with, say, a part of the rigging or, if you are in a wheelhouse, with the edge of one of the windows. Stand and watch if the target changes in relation to this line. This may sound a bit hit and miss, and the boat should be on autopilot to maintain the steady course required, but it can give you a fair idea of any change in the bearing.

You can do much the same with the radar by putting the variable bearing marker (VBM) on the target and seeing if the target moves in relation to that line. Again, it helps if the boat is being steered by autopilot. You should also bear in mind that you are looking for a significant change in the bearing of the other vessel.

Now you need to interpret what constitutes the wording in the rules 'appreciably change'. As a rough guess I

A composite radar picture of the Dover Straits showing the complex shipping picture in these bust shipping lanes

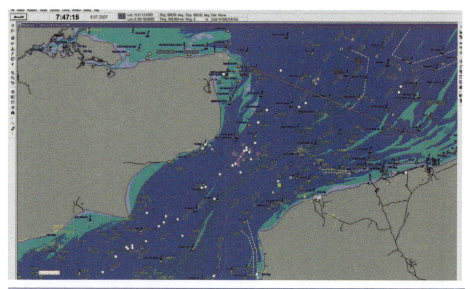

66 PRACTICAL NAVIGATION

COLLISION AVOIDANCE

A developing situation where two ships are involved

When overtaking, the ship ahead may not be aware of your approach astern

would say that you want a change of at least 20° over a few minutes to be on the safe side. If the approaching vessel is a fast boat, you will need a quick change in bearing over a short period of time and with any approaching vessel you should make the assumption that there will be a collision risk until it is clearly proved otherwise.

Take action

The Colregs then tell you who is the give way vessel and who is required to stand so that you don't both try to alter course at the same time.

There is one exception to this; when the two vessels are meeting end on or nearly end on, both are required to alter course to starboard to keep clear of each other. This tends to be one of the most frequent types of encounter when navigating along a coastline or in a channel, where vessels are all on much the same course or reciprocal courses.

In most situations you will not alter course to port when taking avoidance action. This is partly because a vessel on your port side will be the give-way vessel according to the Colregs and partly because if you are giving way to a vessel on your starboard side you don't want to cross their bow. Crossing the bow of any vessel is out of the question in collision avoidance because it increases the risk of the action. It is also important not to let a situation develop where the two craft involved are getting so close that the time available to take avoidance action becomes very limited. Always take any action before the vessels involved get within a mile of each other; this way there is still time to take further action if things do not turn out as planned.

Crowded waters

It is not difficult to see how the situation could become quite complicated even with just two vessels involved. In crowded waters it can become much more so. You might alter course to avoid one vessel only to find that you are then in a collision risk situation with another.

Small craft can be highly manoeuvrable, which makes taking avoidance action fairly simple but you still need to keep your wits about you and remember that slowing down or stopping is a valid option to give yourself time to decide how best to proceed.

It is always quicker and easier to make an assessment of the collision risk situation visually than on a radar display; a good look out is, as ever, key. Complex software now exists for big ships, and this can do most of the sums and recommend appropriate action. The argument over which makes the better decision, the computer or the human, remains unresolved but the Colregs certainly make no allowances for computer generated decisions about collision avoidance.

Overtaking

- If you are an overtaking vessel, it is your job to keep clear of the vessel being overtaken.
- If you are being overtaken, you should maintain your course and speed whilst the other vessel goes past.

COLLISION AVOIDANCE

High speed vessels can pose a significant danger for collision avoidance

This is fine in the open sea but can be a challenge when you are navigating a river or narrow channel and have to alter to keep within the channel. Again, common sense should dictate your actions.

- If you are a small vessel and the other vessel is a ship, you have significantly more room to manoeuvre and should, therefore, give way.
- In narrow channels always keep to the starboard side of the channel as far as possible.

Fast vessels

Common sense must also prevail when a fast vessel and a slow vessel are involved in a potential collision situation.

Fast vessels may be doing 30 knots plus, and this can also apply to the new generation of high-speed ferries that thunder along at up to 40 knots. A 5 knot angling boat may be the give way vessel but the time available for it to take action could be very limited. This can be a difficult situation to cope with and the best solution is to try and navigate away from waters where such fast vessels may operate.

If the fast boat is navigating by radar you might not show up on its radar until it is only a couple of miles away and then there may be only a minute or two for action.

Collision avoidance using radar

First of all, it is worth repeating that if your boat is fitted with radar, the Colregs require you use it.

Variable bearing marker

The simple solution is to use the variable bearing marker (VBM) to check whether a risk of collision exists.

- If the target moves between the VBM and the heading marker, the target will pass ahead of you.
- If it moves away from both the heading marker and the VBM and down the display, it will pass astern.

Relying on radar

If you are trusting the radar on its own as a collision avoidance tool, as could happen in fog, you will want any change in this relative bearing to be considerable before you think about taking action. I have a certain nervousness about altering course using radar alone and the Colregs corroborate this to a certain extent, stating:

'Assumptions shall not be made on the basis of scanty information especially scanty radar information.'

The need for caution is reinforced by some of the problems that can be found with small craft radar. Firstly, there is no guarantee that the radar will pick up every target around you, especially small craft such as RIBs and sailboats with a poor radar return. The problem can get worse if there are waves, as the radar return from the waves might be just as strong as that from any small boats in the vicinity.

Sea clutter

You can turn down the sea clutter to reduce the strength of the returns from the waves but this also effectively reduces the strength of the return from any small craft in the vicinity. Modern radars use advanced software to try to reduce this problem, examining the returns from each tiny area around the vessel and reducing or eliminating any that do show up consistently.

COLLISION AVOIDANCE

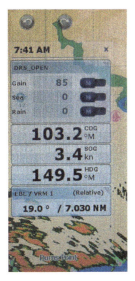

Most radars can have their gain and clutter levels set manually to match the radar to the weather and sea conditions

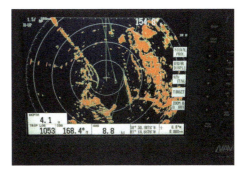

A well adjusted radar that gives a clear picture around you

This should help to eliminate the wave returns because, unlike vessel returns, they tend to be transient. However, it is never going to be 100% foolproof.

Rain clutter

Another potential issue when using radar is rain clutter. In a thunderstorm, and even in light drizzle, the sensitivity of the radar can be affected to varying degrees, resulting in the loss or intermittent detection of targets. The rain clutter of a thunderstorm could lead to the sudden emergence of a target close at hand, whilst lighter rain could reduce the sensitivity of the radar without you being aware of it. Both rain and sea clutter can lead to the 'scanty' radar information referred to by the Colregs.

Alarms

On most small boat radars it is possible to set an alarm to warn you if a target comes within a pre-determined range. This alarm could certainly serve as an additional warning but my feeling is that if you have to rely on an alarm to warn you that a target has come within your pre-set range, you are not doing your job of keeping a radar lookout adequately. You can set similar alarms on AIS receivers but the same applies.

No alarm can tell you what the target is. It could be a buoy or a beacon just as easily as another vessel. The MARPA (Mini-Automatic Radar Plotting Aid; see below) may be able to provide some sort of clue, as may the AIS by showing the target's speed but a better way to help determine what a target is, is to overlay the radar picture onto the electronic chart display. Most modern equipment allows you to do this. If the radar return is a buoy or a beacon target the radar image will show up in the location of that buoy or beacon on the chart. This is not infallible, because if your radar has a wide beam angle, a small boat in the region of the buoy could merge with the buoy into a single target on the radar display.

If you are using the radar in collision avoidance mode, it is probably best to not use the radar as a chart overlay because the more complex picture can be distracting and small target returns could get lost amongst the chart information.

MARPA

Many small boat radars have a Mini-Automatic Radar Plotting Aid (MARPA), which can help you to determine the course and speed of targets detected by the radar. It can even tell you the target's CPA (Closest Point of Approach). This should give an instant indication as to whether any target you select presents a collision risk. It is similar to the system found on the radars of big ships. These do the same thing using Automatic Radar Plotting Aid (ARPA). The principal difference is that ARPA carries out this analysis with every target identified,

COLLISION AVOIDANCE

A dual range radar display is great for collision avoidance

> **How do you tell if your MARPA is sea or ground stabilised?**
> - Find a place where the tide is running and where there is a buoy or other fixed object close by.
> - Locate the buoy on the radar at a suitable range scale and then stop the boat and allow it to drift with the tide.
> - Ping the buoy target with MARPA
> - If the buoy remains more or less stationary on the radar whilst the GPS shows an apparent speed over the ground, the radar is ground stabilised.
> - If, however, the buoy appears to be moving in the opposite direction to the tide and at the speed of the tide according to MARPA, the radar is sea stabilised and ready for using MARPA to its best advantage.
>
> Checks on a number of modern radars showed them all to be ground stabilised

whilst MARPA requires you to select the specific target and can only cope with a certain number of targets.

In theory MARPA should do much of the work when dealing with targets but, as ever when using electronics, it has its drawbacks. Firstly, there will be a delay between you selecting a target and the radar showing what should be a reliable result. This is because the radar takes some time to acquire the average course and speed of the target from which to do its calculations. The longer the target is assessed, the more accurate the results are likely to be.

For MARPA to work it you need to be going at a consistent course and speed. Maintaining a consistent speed should not be a problem, except perhaps on a sailboat where wind gusts or lulls might affect it, whilst running on autopilot should keep a consistent course.

Sea stabilisation

One hidden problem associated with MARPA relates to the speed input of your craft. This input to the radar should be the speed and course through the water, not the speed and course over the ground.

However, you are likely to find that the normal input for the system is the speed and course over the ground (SOG) because these are the most easily obtained from the GPS.

For speed and course through the water, known as sea stabilisation, you need a good quality log and compass with the readout from the latter showing the true rather than the magnetic course. You can use your handbook to work out how to switch to sea stabilisation mode, although this can be tricky.

The difference between ground and sea stabilisation is less of a problem for faster craft, typically those doing over 12 knots, but for sailboats and many slower motor boats it can affect the MARPA considerably and produce unreliable results. It is, however, something you will need to bear in mind even in a faster boat if, for example, you reduce your speed in fog. The difference is caused by the effect of the tide and current on the speed of the boat. It will, therefore, be a problem mainly in northern Europe rather than in the Mediterranean, where there is virtually no tide and only minor currents, and the difference between ground and sea stabilisation should be small.

When navigating on a slow boat in tidal areas, AIS may give you more reliable information about another vessel's course

COLLISION AVOIDANCE

Make sure your navigation lights are in order so others can see you at night

and speed. However, this information is also ground stabilised and will not give a reliable indication of the all-important CPA, which is what you need for collision avoidance. Using that VBM line on the target to establish any change in the relative bearing is still a good indication of whether risk of collision exists.

Make yourself visible

It is important that you can be seen by other vessels. You look out of the wheelhouse window and assume that because you can see the other vessels they can see you. In daylight this should be a fair assumption although small boats can be lost from sight in rough seas.

At night, however, their ability to see you is very much dependent on your navigation lights working as they should. Sometimes a problem can be caused by a flag at the stern that hides the stern navigation light or causes

The white sails of a yacht are not always easily visible in some conditions

it to flicker, other times it is people standing on a flybridge, hiding the masthead light.

Be aware of anything that could obscure the lights on your vessel and make sure that you are as visible as possible.

Summary

The use of electronics for collision avoidance is certainly complex. What seems to be a quick and easy solution to the problem is, in fact, anything but simple.

By all means use the information offered by electronics for collision avoidance but not at the expense of the basics.

Keeping a good visual lookout and acting on the information that you see in the outside world is still the most reliable method of collision avoidance.

Never assume that the other vessel has seen you and will do what is expected of it according to the Colregs.

It is surprising how many skippers, once freed from the shackles of the shore decide that they can relax, enjoy a drink and let the rest of the world go by. I came across this in the Mediterranean where a power yacht on the port side took no avoidance action. I slowed to let it cross my bow and there was no sign of any life on board at all, no lookout and no action, so never take anything for granted.

The Colregs are a masterpiece of regulation covering every possible aspect of navigation at sea. Knowing their content intimately is vitally important if you are going to navigate safety. In some areas they are very precise and in others they are suitably vague; at the end of the day it is you, the skipper, who has to take action in a common sense and seamanlike way. There is no sense in maintaining your course and speed and having a collision simply because you were in the right. Nobody wins in that situation.

The next chapter looks at the special circumstances that cover navigating at night and in poor visibility and this will have particular regard to the particular collision avoidance requirements in those more challenging circumstances.

7 Fog and night navigation

If you find yourself in the unfortunate situation of having to navigate in fog, you will need to be on high alert and raise your concentration levels considerably. You could be forgiven for thinking that with modern electronic systems, much of the challenge of navigating in fog would have disappeared. Electronics, and GPS in particular, have certainly made it less testing but, as always with this wonderful technology, an element of doubt remains.

In the last chapter I looked at some of the weak points of radar and AIS when used for collision avoidance, these weaknesses become much more serious when you have no visual clues to back them up. In fog there is, naturally, a great temptation to put increased faith in the electronics. Knowing their limitations, however, you could be in for some nasty surprises if you rely on them completely and the visual lookout, however restricted, should be maintained.

Fog forecasting

It is not easy to forecast fog because subtle differences in the temperature and moisture content of the atmosphere are sufficient to create it. The required changes can be very local and even over the distance of just a few hundred metres the fog can be patchy and sporadic. On land the subtle changes in temperature and humidity can be measured and detected fairly easily, but fog at sea is much more difficult to forecast reliably because the measurements tend to be harder to obtain and may be more short term in nature. It is, therefore, difficult to take fog into account in your planning. In an ideal world you would avoid fog completely but the uncertainty in its prediction means that there will always be times when you come across it at sea and simply have to cope with it.

White yachts looming out of the fog in a harbour

Fog may only affect some parts of a harbour

FOG AND NIGHT NAVIGATION

Radiation fog

If you are in harbour and wake up to find fog, you may choose to avoid it by waiting for it to clear before setting out. Early morning fog is known as radiation fog and tends to be found in calm conditions, when the land has cooled during the night, causing the moisture in the air to condense and form the tiny droplets of water suspended in the air that constitute fog. Radiation fog will tend to clear when the sun gets up and starts to warm the air and the land; you will often find that the fog has cleared by 10 o'clock, leaving you with a fine warm day in which to continue your sailing.

Radiation fog is unlikely to extend very far out to sea, perhaps just a few miles at most, so if you feel brave enough you might like to feel your way out of harbour to enjoy the clear areas of sea outside. Using electronic charts and GPS with care and discretion, keeping a high standard of lookout, and proceeding slowly, you should be able to navigate through the radiation fog to leave most harbours without any problems. Broadcasts from the harbour radio ought to keep you informed of traffic movements but the service cannot always be relied upon; a high standard of radar watch with the radar on a short range is, therefore, necessary.

Any traffic is likely to be in the form of local vessels, such as harbour ferries or fishing boats, but heading out to sea in these conditions still requires all hands on deck to keep a look out 'by all means possible'. Because of the high level of concentration needed, you will probably breathe a sigh of relief once the fog begins to clear but be sure to remain completely alert until it has fully lifted.

It is possible that rather than awakening to radiation fog, you arrive at your destination harbour, perhaps after an overnight passage, to find it under a blanket of fog. The best solution here is to find an anchorage away from the foggy area and any shipping channels and wait until the harbour radio tells you it has cleared. Alternatively, you could try moving on to another harbour. This is where radio contact or even a mobile phone can be such useful navigation tools. Entering an unknown harbour in fog is not something you want to undertake lightly, unless it is a very straightforward harbour enclosed by a breakwater, with no hard-to-spot buoys marking the channels. Even then you should clear your action with the port authorities who will be able to help with information on other craft movements in the harbour. Much will depend on how poor the visibility is, bearing in mind that radiation fog can be the worst as far as this is concerned. Some buoys are fitted with a wave-actuated bell that will sound as a fog signal. However, for the bell to sound, these must be moving in waves, so you are unlikely to hear any signal in the calm conditions of radiation fog.

Advection fog

The other main fog type that you can encounter at sea is advection fog, which is not found in the open sea. It is easy to assume that fog and calm conditions go hand in hand, but advection fog is different;

Type of fog	Areas affected	Factors for formation	Factors for dispersal
Radiation fog	Inland and harbour areas where the surrounding land is low-lying and moist	Cooling due to radiation from the ground on clear nights when the wind is light. Usually a feature of Anti-cyclone weather	Dispersed when the sun's heat warms the ground or when there is an increase in the wind strength
Advection fog	Sea and adjacent coasts and penetrate into harbours. Also in open seas where cold water exists	Cooling of warm moist air when it comes into contact with the cooler seas	Usually disperses when the wind direction changes. Can also be dispersed near coasts when the sun warms the land/sea

PRACTICAL NAVIGATION

FOG AND NIGHT NAVIGATION

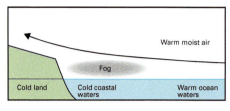

Ships looming up out of the fog at short range can be a scary experience

it needs wind to help it to form. It typically occurs when a warm, moist wind encounters an area of colder sea. The lower temperature of the seawater causes the temperature of the warm air to drop and this in turn causes the moisture to condense and form the fog. It can be somewhat unsettling to find yourself sailing along in a lively sea, surrounded by thick fog. Fortunately, advection fog is easier to forecast than radiation fog because the wind direction and moisture content, along with the sea temperatures, should be known. However, when it comes to fog nothing is ever certain. Advection fog will tend to clear when the sea temperature rises or, more commonly, when the wind direction changes. It is likely to be found in areas such as the English Channel, when a warm, moist south westerly encounters colder seas further up channel and it is in the winter months that the conditions required for its formation are most prevalent.

Collision avoidance

Collision avoidance, a topic covered in detail in the previous chapter, is probably the biggest challenge in foggy conditions. When seeking to avoid collisions in fog you will need to place a much higher reliance on the radar because it can 'see' where you can't. A whole new set of Colregs come into play when navigating in fog.

Rule 19 - The conduct of vessels in reduced visibility, applies to vessels out of sight of one another when navigating in or near an area of restricted visibility. Restricted visibility is defined as visibility reduced by fog, mist, falling snow, heavy rainstorms or showers, sand storms or any similar causes.

The rule requires you to proceed at a safe speed, suitable for the prevailing conditions, but does not go on to define what constitutes this safe speed. A safe speed is sometimes defined as one where you can stop in half the

Radar reflectors on buoys can make them more distinctive on radar

distance of the visibility range. This makes sense to a certain degree because another approaching vessel will travel into that visibility zone at the same time, so you both need to be able to stop before you hit one another. However, this 'half the visibility' range speed does not allow any time for detecting the other vessel or for taking the action needed to slow the vessel, so an even slower speed would be safer. You might want to test just how long it takes your boat to stop at various speeds to gain an idea of what might be a safe speed in fog.

Radar in fog

The Colregs go into some detail on the use of radar in fog.

You are allowed to alter course based on radar information alone, provided that you do so in good time and do not alter course to port unless the other vessel is approaching from the starboard quarter.

As you might expect, the matter does become complicated. It is much the same with the sound signals that you are required to make, according to the sort of vessel you

FOG AND NIGHT NAVIGATION

FOG OPERATION CHECKLIST

Measuring the visibility
You can only measure the visibility accurately when you have another object in sight, so assume that it is poorer than you think. It can take time to 'see' another vessel as you may not be looking directly at it when it first appears.

Speed in fog
Ensure you are able to stop in half the distance of the visibility because a conflicting vessel will need a similar distance to stop. Proceed slowly.

Keeping a lookout
Post a crew member to keep a visual lookout, preferably stationed outside, as you will be busy monitoring the radar and the chart plotter as well as trying to keep a lookout.

Using radar
Radar is an important aid in fog but don't expect it to pick up all the vessels around you, particularly when the sea is lively and wave clutter obstructs the centre of the display, obscuring small vessels.

Using the autopilot
The autopilot can be vital in fog as it saves you having to concentrate on the steering and allows you to focus on navigation. Make sure you know where the disconnect button is in case you need manual steering in a hurry.

Navigation in fog
You will not get many visual clues in fog, so you will be heavily reliant on the chart plotter and/or the radar. Use both, together with the depth sounder, for a triple check on your position.

Types of fog
Radiation fog occurs early in the morning, mainly in harbours, and should clear when the sun warms things up.

Advection fog is found at sea when warm, moist air flows over a cold sea and needs a change of wind direction or sea temperature before clearing.

Sailing in fog
Ideally you should not be under sail in fog. You may not be able to manoeuvre quickly, the sail can obstruct visibility, and white sails will not show up.

Safety margins
Allow greater safety margins in fog, particularly for making a landfall. Moderate your speed so you can stop or take avoiding action in good time.

Make your boat more visible
Have the navigation lights on, even in daylight. If you have a searchlight, have this turned on as well, facing forward. The radar reflector should be up and working.

You need to concentrate on the visual lookout in fog

PRACTICAL NAVIGATION

FOG AND NIGHT NAVIGATION

are in. If you hear the fog signal of another vessel apparently forward of your beam, you must reduce speed to the minimum needed to maintain steerageway and navigate with extreme caution until the danger of collision is over. I cannot recollect when I last heard a sound signal in fog, big ships certainly rarely use them these days, but if things do go wrong when you are navigating in fog and you are not sounding fog signals, the blame is likely to fall on you. Bear in mind that you are unlikely to hear the signals if you are inside a wheelhouse and that they can also be drowned out by the noise of a running engine.

Radar antennae

Most small boat radars have a small antenna. The beam width of the radar is directly related to the diameter of the rotating scanner.

You may find beam widths of around 5° which means that anything picked up by the radar on the same range within that 5° sector will show up as a single target. Some radars extend the beam width out to 7° and a wide beam width can make finding a harbour entrance a challenge. If that entrance is between two breakwaters, the opening will not show up until you are quite close because both ends of the breakwater are within that wide beam width and look like a continuous target.

Another factor to consider as regards the radar antenna is where it is mounted. On a motorboat this might be on a low arch mast at the rear of the flybridge but beware that crew standing up there can block the radar signal ahead, with potentially serious consequences. I have experienced this when approaching a harbour with a long breakwater and just a narrow break for the entrance. It was night and I was on the radar in the wheelhouse with the rest of the crew on the flybridge. I could see the gap in the breakwater ahead and urged them on only to suddenly hear the engines go into full reverse. My 'gap' in the breakwater was in fact created by the crew blocking the radar signal ahead!

Entering fog

When approaching or moving into fog, you are essentially entering into a different navigation mode. It is very much a case of 'all hands on deck'. You will need help with the visual lookout, help to maintain a constant watch on the radar and help to prepare the boat for fog operations. You need to make your boat as visible as possible; switch on your navigation lights and any other bright lights on deck, even in daylight. Seeing as many other vessels out there will be navigating on radar alone, having the radar reflector turned on goes without saying. If you have invested in a radar target enhancer that transmits a signal to make your radar more visible, so much the better. AIS can also be used to make your boat more detectable and to also detect other vessels fitted with AIS but you must remember that not all vessels will have the system.

Fog can play some strange visual tricks

FOG AND NIGHT NAVIGATION

Expect the unexpected in fog; like this temporary drilling rig

A buoy shows up well once it is close but it can be challenging to get that first sighting

Maintain a lookout

If the design of your boat allows, you should keep your lookout from outside. On most sailboats this will be automatic, as you are in the cockpit, but on a motorboat the flybridge is better than the wheelhouse. Positioning yourself outside will allow you to hear any sound signals but, more importantly, you will see any approaching vessels much sooner because your sight will be focussed on what is around you at sea, rather than on the distractions of the wheelhouse.

If you have the crew available and the conditions allow, station someone in the bow where there will be an unrestricted view ahead.

Maintaining a lookout in fog can be very challenging as there may be nothing specific to focus on through the whiteness. It becomes very easy to imagine you see something ahead when there is nothing there at all. Equally, it can take some time to focus on another vessel emerging from the fog and to be confident that there really is another vessel there.

Sailboats in fog

On a sailboat you are probably better off navigating with the sails down. The foresails can obstruct the view ahead and the normal white sails do not show up well in fog. Under sail you have less scope to manoeuvre in an emergency and no astern gear for an emergency stop.

- Use your autopilot for steering if you have one as this will not only relieve the need for someone to be on the wheel and focussing on the compass but it will also help maintain a steady course; a great help when trying to get a steady and easy to interpret radar picture. When using the autopilot, if you have one with a rotary knob course control, you can use this for any quick alterations but you should also know where the standby button is so you can quickly disconnect when manual steering is required.

The stand-by button on an autopilot needs highlighting for quick action

- If possible, assign a dedicated crewmember to the radar so that he or she can focus on that alone and assess the risks.

- If you don't have the crew numbers to do this, set up alarms so that you will at least get an audible warning if anything comes within a certain range around you.

- You can do the same with the sounder, which can be very useful if you are making a landfall in fog, without the electronic chart to help.

Making a landfall in fog

Prior to the advent of GPS and electronic charts there were various techniques used when making a landfall in fog.

One of these was to set a landfall point to one side of your planned destination so as to

PRACTICAL NAVIGATION 77

FOG AND NIGHT NAVIGATION

> **COLREG requirements**
>
> In addition to the standard requirements, the following Colregs rules apply to poor visibility:
>
> You are required to proceed at a 'safe speed' adapted to the state of the visibility
>
> Your speed should also be determined by the characteristics, efficiency and limitations of the radar equipment on board and the possibility that small vessels may not be detected at an adequate range
>
> You must use your radar if it is fitted but do not make assumptions from scanty radar information
>
> You must have your navigation lights on in restricted visibility
>
> A yacht over 12 metres in length is required to have a bell and a whistle for sound signals. Under 12 metres other means of making sound signals may be used.
>
> Appropriate sound signals must be made when in or near restricted visibility

know which way to turn to find your destination when you did sight land. If using this technique, try to choose a landfall point that is easily recognisable so that you will know it when you see it. I have had locals on board who swore they knew every inch of the coast and would recognise each bit of land we sighted...All well and good, except they didn't recognise it and we didn't know which way to turn for the harbour entrance. On that occasion I took the boat back offshore, ran along the coast for a while and then tried another landfall point but there was still no sign of recognition from the 'local knowledge' on board. It was getting dark and we could see lights on the shore so we landed with the tender and finally asked in a pub to find out where we were!

Another technique when navigating in fog is to approach the coastline at an angle so that you only have to turn through a relatively small angle to get out of danger rather than the 180° that you might have to turn if you approach the coastline head on.

With an electronic chart and GPS on board you might not feel the need to take these precautions but it is still important to have a more cautious approach because in fog you will little or no means of making visual checks on your course and progress.

You can use the radar for checking your position and it is wise to set a range ring or an alarm as a check when approaching a coast or headland, along with the sounder when approaching shallow water.

As always with navigation, you need to use all means possible to check out your position and your progress. Making a landfall on electronics alone can be a nervous time until you make that vital visual contact. Small boat radars with their wide beam angle do not always present the clear picture that you would like, so should be used with a bit more caution.

With advection fog there is the possibility that the fog will clear to a degree when you approach land as the water temperature may rise under the influence of the land.

Night navigation

There are many similarities between navigating in fog and navigating at night. Both scenarios take you out of your comfort zone and require you to work that bit harder as you adapt your navigation techniques to cope with the changing environment.

The margins for safe navigation are that bit smaller and you need to raise your game to compensate.

At night the navigation environment changes significantly, you are unable to see the waves or the potential wind changes that help guide your navigational decisions in the daylight. Breaking waves in tide races, changes when the wind is against the tide, and the potential increase in wind strength from an advancing squall may all arrive virtually unannounced at night, so it is vital to exercise a higher degree of caution in your navigation. As always, electronic systems can help but they do not offer a complete solution.

Navigation is a lot easier when you can see what is around you and can use visual navigation as a vital check on progress. At night the familiar scene of land, buoys and other navigation marks disappears to be

FOG AND NIGHT NAVIGATION

NIGHT OPERATIONS

Navigation lights
Navigation lights are vital at night – aside from being a mandatory requirement, they are the only way that other vessels can see you. Make sure they are bright and angled appropriately. Fit the largest bulbs possible and make sure that nothing, such as sails or flags, is obstructing them.

Colregs
The collision avoidance regulations (Colregs) apply at night, just as they do in daylight but there are specific requirements for lights. Make sure you know what all the various light signals mean and remember that many vessels, such as fishing vessels and cruise ships, carry lighting that obscures the navigation lights.

Flashing lights
Most buoy and lighthouse lights are flashing in one form or another, which can make it very hard to judge how far you are away from them. Take extra care when judging distances at night.

Check battery charge
On a motorboat battery charge is not a problem but under sail the battery drain can be considerable, so keep an eye on the charge of the battery during a night sail.

Autopilot
Using the autopilot at night gives a steady course so flashing lights appear in the same point on the horizon at each flash, making them easier to see and identify. Make sure you know where the 'off' switch is on the autopilot so you can use it in a hurry.

Sailing at night
Operating under sail at night adds to the challenge. You will only have the sidelights on, making it harder for other vessels to see you, and the sails can obstruct large parts of your visible horizon.

Safety margins
Allow extra safety margins at night and try to keep out of the main shipping channels so that you have less collision avoidance to worry about.

Shore lights
Navigating at night against a backdrop of bright shore lights can be challenging. Ships and buoys can be hard to detect and the bright lights can affect your 'night vision'.

---

replaced by fixed and flashing lights. After dark everything is in code. There is no quick fix for this and you have to decipher the meaning of the lights before you can understand what you are seeing. This adds considerably to the workload of the navigator at a time when you may already be feeling the pressure of having to sail the boat in the dark anyway. Night navigation is challenging but there are ways to simplify things if you get organised.

Radar at night
When navigating at night you can exploit the capabilities of radar beyond its usual uses for general navigation and collision avoidance. Radar can detect differences in the surface of the sea from the stronger returns that are found when the seas are rougher. An advancing squall may be detected by the stronger returns from the steeper waves within the squall area and show up as a vague target on the display.

The breaking waves in tide races can also show up quite clearly and give advance warning of approaching danger. I had a good example of this when on the west coast of Ireland, passing through a narrow channel at night in a fast planing boat. We were well through the channel when I saw an unexplained rough-edged target ahead. Realising that it was probably an area of breaking waves, I shouted to the skipper to slow down, which we did just in time before we entered the steep waves of the tide race. If you have the chance, look for these possible radar targets in the daytime when you can see what is ahead of you, you will then be better able to interpret what you are seeing at night.

FOG AND NIGHT NAVIGATION

Land features can be very indistinct at night

Use autopilot

The first step is to use the autopilot for steering. Not only does this relieve you of the job of steering the boat by hand and peering at the compass, which can destroy your night vision, but it also stabilises the view from the boat. One of the biggest problems that you can face at night is that of the boat swinging about, as you are quite likely to steer a somewhat erratic course. With autopilot steering on, the lights you are using as navigation references remain in the same part of the horizon and on a steady course, so a flashing light is easier to find and check.

When the autopilot is steering the boat the radar display is also stabilised, so you will have a much better picture for both navigation and collision avoidance. Buoys and other boats and ships will stay in the same place on the screen in the short term and it will be much easier to relate them to the lights that you see outside. It also means that getting a relative bearing of targets is a viable means of checking for collision risk.

Shore lights can present a confusing picture at night

Plan your route

The basic method of navigating at night is much the same as navigation in daylight.

- Do your passage planning and work out the course that you want to follow, either on the paper or the electronic chart
- Mark the waypoints where the course will be altered
- Check the route in detail to ensure that you are not passing close or even over the top of any dangers.

Once these initial steps are done it is time to look at adapting your navigation plan to make night navigation easier and safer.

Identify lights

The first thing to do is look along the route to see where there are navigation lights to provide you with that vital visual check that the electronic systems are giving you reliable information. Even now, when the number of lights is being cut back, there are still enough left out there to ensure that you will have at least one lighthouse in sight when navigating along a coastline.

Trying to identify lights at night can be a real challenge. They flash with different characteristics to enable identification but

Twilight can be a challenge as navigation lights are less clear and shore features are lost

FOG AND NIGHT NAVIGATION

These ship lights are not easy to see against the shore lights

trying to peer at the chart and see which lights are relevant can be challenging when, as you may find along a buoyed channel, there are several flashing lights in view. It can be hard to read the small print on the chart when the boat is bouncing around in waves, so ring them with a pencil on the paper chart and note the characteristics of the light so that you can check them at a glance. On the electronic chart you can usually discover light characteristics by clicking on the light icon, revealing a pop-up box with the details.

Adjust your course

You might also wish to adjust the course you set, to make life easier at night. Rather than take the direct route between waypoints, it may be beneficial to take a course that passes close to a buoy or some other mark with a light. This will give you a positive position check as you pass.

If you are steering manually, having a light ahead or nearly ahead to steer on is also much easier than trying to steer a compass course.

However, avoid steering directly towards a buoy light because it is incredibly difficult to judge distances from a flashing light at night and you may suddenly find yourself much closer to the buoy than you intended, particularly if the tide is flowing with you.

If the tide is not directly behind you, watch out for it setting you down towards the buoy. I have had one or two near misses by not realising just how close I was to a buoy at night, so make sure that the bearing of the buoy is opening up as you get closer to ensure that you will pass well clear of it when it is abeam.

Scan the horizon

When keeping a visual lookout for other vessels around you, make a slow scan of the horizon rather than a quick glance. Small craft may be moving up and down in waves making their lights look like a navigation mark whilst the flashing lights of buoys may only show up at intervals.

The often small, faint lights that might signal a small boat can be hard to pick out at a glance so a concentrated lookout is vital. If you are the only person on watch, you will have a full-time job.

You will have to scan the horizon for lights, monitor the navigation and steer the boat, although, as mentioned, the task can be made a little easier by using the autopilot whenever possible.

The temptation will always be to focus on the electronic screens because these are the most interesting things in view. There is no doubt that they give you a lot of the information you need for navigating the boat safely but there is no guarantee that they will show everything that is out there. Be prudent and keep up the visual lookout even at night.

Avoid other vessels

For collision avoidance at night you must know the Colregs and understand what all the different lights on ships and boats mean. Unless it is coming directly towards you, the lights will not give you the precise heading of another vessel that they would provide in the daytime. Watching the bearing of the other vessel and how it changes is vital. Even more vital is to note when the bearing of the other vessel is not changing and there is a collision risk. You will have to take appropriate action to avoid danger (see the previous chapter for further information on this).

Navigation lights are your only guide as to the type of vessel and its heading at night

FOG AND NIGHT NAVIGATION

Understand navigation lights

The requirements for navigation lights at night, as dictated by the Colregs, are far from perfect and a single white light could mean many things; a stern light of a ship, a small boat, or an anchor light. You can be quite close before you spot the weak light from a small boat and it can be hard to judge the distance, so, as in the daytime, constant vigilance is vital in crowded waters.

Keep an eye out for the high lights at the top of the masthead on a sailboat; these can be easily missed when looking out towards the horizon.

Also make sure that your own navigation lights are in good order so other craft can see you. As when navigating in fog, beware of stern lights partly concealed by flags and white masthead lights blocked by crewmembers at the helm of small craft.

Note also that the location of lights on small craft does not always conform to the Colreg requirements.

Dim electronic displays

When using electronic equipment at night, dim the displays and dials in the cockpit to avoid being dazzled and losing your night vision. The chances are that you will spend more time looking at the displays at night because they tend to present a more interesting picture than the horizon but they should be dimmed as far as possible to reduce glare. Bits of sticky tape can help to cut down the brightness of indicator lights on the dashboard that cannot be dimmed.

The lights from the dashboard can affect your night vision and be distracting

When choosing electronic equipment it is important to make sure that it is not only the screen that lights up at night but also the control buttons. If you have to get a torch out every time you want to alter a setting it will not only take your mind off the navigation itself but also destroy your night vision. Having the autopilot standby switch clearly illuminated so that you can find it quickly in the dark is vital.

Entering harbour

The most challenging part of night navigation tends to be entering harbour. A big lighthouse at a harbour entrance will hopefully show up well against the shore lights and serve as a guide to help you find the entrance channel. However, if you have to pick out a buoy light against the shore lights it can be a real struggle to find and you can be confused by neon and other flashing lights on the shore. Once you have found the first fairway buoy it will be easier to locate the others against the shore lights because you will know approximately where to look.

Shore lights can also make it difficult to identify the weak lights of small craft. The radar can be a great help here but, as we have already said, radar cannot be guaranteed to pick up every small vessel, so the visual lookout is vital. The Colregs require you to proceed at a safe speed and the 'presence of background light such as from shore lights' is one of the factors that has to be taken into account in determining

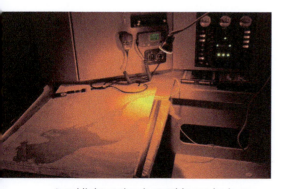

A red light at the chart table can be better to help retain your night vision

FOG AND NIGHT NAVIGATION

The visual lookout at night is vital to see weak lights ahead

what constitutes this safe speed. You are better off navigating from the flybridge on a motorboat if it is an option.

On sailboats it makes sense to take down sails to give a clearer view when entering harbour and it could be good practice to have a lookout on the bow.

The electronic chart can be very valuable when entering harbours at night. The GPS should be accurate enough to at least position you in the entrance channel and show a plan view of an unfamiliar harbour. The accuracy level may not be high enough for detailed harbour navigation so do not rely on it entirely but it can be a considerable aid to sorting out the various features of the harbour. When navigating in harbours at night, it will be easier if you have the tide ebbing underneath you. This will enable you to stop and work things out rather than having a flood tide driving you inexorably into the harbour.

Navigating at night can stretch your navigation skills and in addition to careful planning you need an even higher level of concentration than in daytime. The reward is the great sense of achievement that you will feel when you make harbour after a successful night passage.

- Using the autopilot can reduce the workload and enable you to keep a steadier course.

- Always check the electronic positions with visual checks when possible.

- Have the characteristics of navigation lights readily available for reference before you start out

- Remember it can be difficult to judge distances at night.

- Electronics can help considerably but do not rely on them totally. Avoid over-reliance on radar in particular.

- Remember that spotting the lights of other yachts against the shore lights can be challenging.

- Make sure that your lights are working properly and are not concealed by any obstructions.

There can be many confusing lights on shore at night which could hide moving vessels and navigation marks

8 Navigation under sail

When navigating under sail, there are four kinds of information that you can use to improve efficiency and safety.

Firstly there is *measured* information, and the information that can be *calculated* from this. Next there is information that is *estimated* or what we might call intelligent guesswork. Finally there is *forecast* information.

Gathering the necessary information to sail at maximum efficiency is a complex business, which is why good sailboat navigators are very much in demand amongst the racing fraternity. For some cruising sailors, efficient navigation can become an obsession, as they seek to acquire all the possible information to work out the best and quickest route possible. However, most sailors are just out there to enjoy their sail and will make their judgements by the seat of their pants, using their experience to get the best out of their sailing. I sail a 110 year old gaff rig sailboat where there are no electronics at all and we sail and navigate simply by using our judgement. We may not be the fastest on the water but it gives us tremendous satisfaction when we get it right. This chapter looks at each of these four information types in turn in order to gain a clearer understanding of navigation under sail.

SAILBOAT PERFORMANCE PARAMETERS

MEASURED
Position
Boat speed
Speed over the ground (SOG)
Compass heading
Course over the ground (COG)
Apparent wind direction
Apparent wind speed
Depth
Polar diagram

CALCULATED
True wind speed
True wind direction
Wind trends, speed and direction.
Velocity made good (VMG)
Course made good (CMG)
Lay line
Tide and leeway effects
Cross track error (CTE)
Depth trends

ESTIMATED
Tide speed and direction
Leeway

FORECAST
Wind speed and direction changes
Associated sea conditions
The set and rate of the tide
The height of the tide

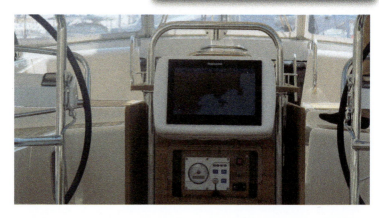

A typical navigation screen installation in a sailboat cockpit

84 PRACTICAL NAVIGATION

NAVIGATION UNDER SAIL

Measured information

Measured information, provided by instruments found on board the boat, will provide you with basic information on performance.

1. Speed through water and over ground

The log can measure your speed through the water and thereby give a measure of how efficiently the boat is sailing. The better the sails are utilising the available wind power, the faster the speed through the water.

Speed over the ground, meanwhile, is derived from the relative GPS positions. This is easy to measure as it is automatically calculated on the chart plotter display.

2. Direction

Information on direction can be obtained from the compass. This will give you the heading of the yacht as it is being steered but to be useful and compatible with the GPS direction it will need to be converted to a true heading. The direction derived from the GPS is known as the course made good; tides and leeway mean this will usually be different to the compass heading.

3. Wind

The masthead sensors show the speed and direction of the 'apparent' wind. This is the wind that powers you along when under sail and is what you actually feel blowing across the boat. It combines the actual wind with the movement of the boat. Further information on the wind can be obtained from the polar diagram: a projected assessment of the performance of a sailing yacht on various headings in relation to the wind direction and various wind strengths. It is usually produced by the builder or designer of the yacht and can be used to find the most efficient angle of sailing for a particular wind. Most sailors would use this on its own in a manual way but with sophisticated computer programmes the polar diagram can be incorporated into the assessment sailing programme.

Calculated information and electronics

It is from these basic building blocks that you can make your assessment of the conditions and progress in order to optimise the performance. At this stage you may want to step away from the electronic information and use your own assessments to mentally optimise the route and sail setting. However, by feeding electronic information into a computer you can get a much more accurate picture of the performance. Sophisticated software can take a lot of the guesswork out of the navigation equation and help you to optimise the route you take to get to the next waypoint.

1. Refine the information

The first stage of this computerised optimisation is the refinement of the information taken from the various onboard sensors. As always, the accuracy of the output from the computer is only as good as the accuracy of the information that is fed in. The accuracy of the information from the GPS regarding the course and speed over the ground will be as good as it gets and there is little that can be done in terms of refinement here. The compass heading can be made more accurate by using a high-grade fluxgate compass or even one of the new GPS compasses; both of these have become quite sophisticated on modern sailboats.

It is much the same with the autopilots that use this information to maintain the course; the log will need to be calibrated in order to get the most accurate reading of the speed through the water. This can be done by comparing the speed registered by the log to

A basic sailboat display showing wind direction in relation to heading

NAVIGATION UNDER SAIL

that registered by the GPS when under motor at slack water, in still conditions. It should be done over the speed range. Most logs allow you to add these corrections to the log reading so that they are applied automatically, thereby providing you with good quality information to feed into the computer.

Finally, the wind sensors at the masthead will show inaccurate readings when the boat is rolling or pitching. These variations can be averaged out to improve the accuracy of the reading but a more sophisticated solution is to measure the sideways and fore and aft components of the inaccuracy so that it can be removed by suitable software.

2. Use technology to make calculations

Now you have the data from the sensors knocked into suitable shape it is ready to form the basis of the computer calculations. Possible solutions that software can provide are:

- Velocity Made Good (VMG), which is a measure of the performance towards your next waypoint
- Effects of tides and leeway on the progress of the boat
- The establishment of a lay line to the next waypoint or turning mark and when it is okay to tack to follow this line.

Indeed, it can provide information on virtually everything you need to know in order to sail the boat at maximum efficiency. These units take virtually all the guesswork out of high efficiency sailing and can also

Wind and performance information can help in the changeable conditions around a headland

A sailboat information display showing both graphic and numerical information

show you the effects of the wind and tide on your progress, enabling you to note any changes. Take care when using electronic instruments to ensure that you know which units are being displayed. The course may be in true or magnetic form and the speed may be in knots, mph or kph, whilst depths are normally in metres to correspond with the chart but on older units you might find them in feet and fathoms.

Estimated information

Computer systems can tell you how to sail the boat most efficiently to reach a waypoint but they require the most current information about the wind and tide conditions in order to be able to reach their conclusions. If your next waypoint is located off a headland you can find that both wind and tide change significantly on the approach. Both have the potential to increase considerably around a headland, upsetting the careful calculations of the computer. Unfortunately, the computer cannot forecast these changing conditions, this is where your estimation skills come in. A lot will depend on how far off the headland you have decided to place the waypoint and this in turn will probably depend on what you expect the wind and tide to be doing.

1. Wind strength and direction

Forecast charts can give a good idea of the general direction of the wind when sailing away from the land but near the headland conditions will be much harder to predict. As

NAVIGATION UNDER SAIL

Time to look at sailing efficiency when clear of the harbour

Forecast information

1. Wind strength and direction

In a sailboat your navigation is, naturally, restricted by wind direction. There is an arc of about 90°/45°on either side of the wind direction in which you will not make headway, so your navigation options will be limited. Of course you can make headway upwind by tacking, sailing as close as possible to the wind, first on one side and then the other, to progress towards your next waypoint. Most experienced sailors will do this almost by instinct, assessing where and how to make the course changes but electronic systems can also come to your aid. For the cruising sailor there is some satisfaction in optimising your sailing in this way but for the racing sailor, for whom taking the optimum route is vital to success, the assistance of these systems can be essential.

you close the headland, the wind direction and strength can change significantly, particularly if the wind is off the land. You may even find dead areas where the wind has virtually disappeared. When conditions can be so incredibly local, experience and estimation are the only means of preparing.

2. Tidal flow

The same uncertainty is likely to arise with tidal flow. The charts will show you the general direction and strength of the tide but there can be considerable local variations and eddies when you are within a mile or so of the shore. You might want to take an inshore route to try and cheat the tide only to find that you run out of wind. The situation can get even more complex when navigating around a pronounced headland. Until we are able to get much more detailed wind and tide information for these localised areas, which is many, many years away, you will have to rely on your skill and experience to select the best course to follow. Your computer system or competitors working to alternative routes will only be able to tell you whether you made the right choice after the event.

A comprehensive information display that also shows trends in wind direction and speed

A wind forecast chart can provide useful input to the sailing instruments

PRACTICAL NAVIGATION 87

NAVIGATION UNDER SAIL

The vital role played by the strength and direction of the wind when navigating under sail means that accurate, up-to-date wind forecasts are essential. This is where the forecast information comes in. It is never easy to get truly accurate information on forecast winds because forecasts are never more than estimations. There are infinite sources of weather information but many can be rather vague when it comes to the forecasting of wind and the timing of changes. On land, the direction and strength of the wind are not normally considered to be as important as the rain and sunshine, it is advisable, therefore, to use a dedicated marine forecast. However, many of these can also be vague, about both the direction and strength of the wind and whether these changes will be sudden or slow to occur, because they are general forecasts covering large sea areas and tend not to be specific enough for your purpose. There is also a tendency to over-forecast the wind strength in the name of caution.

What you need to know is what the wind will be doing along the route that you propose to follow; will there be any changes during your voyage and, if so, when will they take place. You may have to pay to get the sort of high quality weather information you require but to a certain extent you can also work it out for yourself, probably with better results because you are able to take into account the topography of the coastline along which you are sailing and its possible effects on wind direction and strength.

2. Planning around the wind forecast

The first step is to look at the general weather pattern shown on weather charts that show the pattern of the isobars, the high and low pressure areas and, perhaps most importantly, where the weather fronts are located.

You should watch these weather patterns for several days in advance, to build up a feel for how the weather is developing. The forecast charts will show how fronts are likely to develop in both the short and long term.

From this you will understand the flow of the weather and be able to anticipate how the wind direction is likely to change so that you can choose a sailing direction that takes maximum advantage of the forecast changes in wind direction.

On a route across the English Channel, for example, you could be faced with southerly winds and have to choose a tack on which to set out. If the forecasts suggest

Possible sailing courses can be constrained by nearby shoals

NAVIGATION UNDER SAIL

Clear digital displays can help in adverse conditions

3. Sailing along a coastline

You can use these same tactics when sailing along a coastline, in estuaries, along narrow channels or in the vicinity of an island. However, land features rather complicate matters, as there will be many local factors affecting the wind strength and direction.

- Local turbulence and temperature differences between the sea and the land can both have an effect on the wind and produce notable changes in land and sea breezes.
- The difference in the friction produced by the wind and the land and the wind and the sea surface also has an impact; it can allow the wind to not only increase in strength over the sea but also cause it to veer by up to 30° as it moves out over the water. This land/sea interface can be a complicated area for forecasters and you may not always be sure whether the forecast is giving the wind direction over the sea or over the land.

that the wind is likely to veer, i.e. swing clockwise, as can often be the case, you would want to start out on the starboard tack i.e. eastwards of the direct line. In this way, when the wind veers, the wind direction will become more westerly and you will be able to sail closer to your desired course as the wind changes.

Another situation to take into consideration is when the wind conditions suggest that there will be gusts occurring. Gusts can be fairly frequent when you have disturbed conditions such as the passage of frontal systems but you can also find gusts occurring in quite moderate conditions, particularly when it is raining. Not only does the wind strength increase when you experience a gust but it can also change direction by perhaps 20 or 30°. A direction change will almost always be clockwise in the northern hemisphere. Bear this in mind when selecting the tack for a windward course.

Windforce at sea when coastal winds are onshore	Factor by which to multiply coastal station wind to obtain wind over the sea	
	By day	By night
4	1·1	1·7
5	1·3	1·6
6	1·4	1·8
7	1·3	1·6
8	1·3	1·6
9	no figures	1·6

The wind will always tend to be less over the land than the sea and these tables give the factors by which to multiply the wind strength as given in the reports from coastal stations. They are increased at night becuase wind strength tends to be underestimated on land at night

Windforce at sea when coastal station wind is routed over land	Factor by which to multiply coastal station wind to obtain wind over the sea	
	By day	By night
5	1·2	1·6
6	1·4	1·9
7	1·6	1·6
8	1·7	1·8
9	no figures	1·8

When using this table bear in mind that a high land station could experience a stronger wind than that at sea level and that the wind can be accelerated around headlands

PRACTICAL NAVIGATION

NAVIGATION UNDER SAIL

Matters can become even more complicated when there are high cliffs along the shoreline.

- Considerable eddies can form in wind blowing off the land as it passes over the cliffs and heads out to sea.
- Close inshore you may find that the wind almost reverses direction as the wind flows over the cliff and then turns back to try and fill the semi-vacuum at sea level below the cliffs.
- The turbulence created around cliffs can stretch for up to four miles offshore so you might want to keep clear of this area to make your sailing easier and the wind more reliable.

You can find similarly variable winds when the shoreline consists of alternate cliffs and valleys. Here the wind will be focused on flowing down the valleys so you are likely to find stronger winds at sea when sailing off the valley areas.

Islands and pronounced headlands can also create disturbances. Around islands the airflow tries to go both around and over the island. The effects of this tend to be particularly noticeable on the lee side. Around pronounced headlands, meanwhile, expect to find an increase in the wind strength offshore from the headland. The cause here is compressed airflow; the wind direction will tend to follow the line of the headland for some distance on each side.

These storm clouds herald changes in the wind

Expect to find changes in wind direction and speed as well as in the tides around headlands

None of these localised conditions will be forecast, so it is up to you to make your own assessments.

4. Sea breezes

Sea breezes are another factor that you need to take into account if you are going to navigate with a sailboat in varying wind conditions.

- On warm days when the land heats up more than the sea, the air over the land rises up. As the warmer air rises it draws in cooler air from over the sea. The rising warm air cools as it gets higher and creates a sort of circular air flow, or sea breeze, which can extend three or four miles out to sea.
- On days when there is a fresh breeze running along the coast due to the principal airflow, this main flow can be diverted by the influence of the sea breeze and run, instead at perhaps 45° to the coastline.
- On a fairly calm day the sea breeze will be at more or less 90°, which can make a great wind for sailing across the bay with a beam reach.

5. Wind in channels

In narrow channels you can find that the wind blows directly up or down the channel, irrespective of what the main airflow is doing. This situation tends to be particularly prevalent when there is high land along the sides of the channel. You may be faced with a series of short tacks if you are unfortunate

NAVIGATION UNDER SAIL

In narrow channels expect the wind to be funnelled either up or down the channel

enough to have the wind against you. If the channel is inside an island, it may be worth taking a longer route around the outside in order to get a more favourable wind.

It can be complicated trying to assess all the factors that influence the wind and the resultant conditions that you might face when navigating along a coastline. However, there can be a lot of satisfaction in working out just where the wind will be blowing from and then planning your course to take maximum advantage of the anticipated wind. When cruising, nothing is critical, even when you get it wrong but when you are racing it can make the difference between finishing first and being an also-ran. There ought to be a computer programme that could do the sums for you but there are so many variable factors to take into account and so many elements to estimate that you are probably better off adapting your navigation to the changing circumstances as you go along, rather than trying to anticipate them too far in advance, except in more general terms.

The more general wind changes, such as periods when the wind will veer or back-up due to the general weather patterns, can be anticipated to some extent, and doing so can give you a significant advantage. It is possible with a sailing computer to keep a plot of the wind direction and strength and this should help to give you an indication of the trend in the wind direction. Most skippers are likely to use a combination of electronics and forecasting to achieve the best results for their forecast information.

6. Setting a course upwind

In general terms, when faced with setting a course upwind, you want to make your first tack to the left of the wind direction, i.e. on the starboard tack. If you expect the wind to veer or back-up, make a port tack. Of course there will be exceptions to this rule. A significant one occurs when you are running

A comprehensive polar diagram on computer

Setting a course upwind

1. You could tack out to seaward and, hopefully, find a stronger tide to help you along.
2. You could tack into the bay between the headlands, where the tide should be weaker, important if it is against you, and the seas should be calmer. However, the wind may become more variable and erratic when it is blowing off the adjacent land and you could find yourself facing a head wind as you approach that distant headland. Once again, knowing if the wind is likely to veer or back-up could have a bearing on your choice.
3. Alternatively proceed across the bay in a series of relatively short tacks
4. Or, set off taking longer tacks, steadily shortening them as you get close to your waypoint. This way you will not get badly put out if the expected shifts or changes do not occur and you will only be a short distance away from the lay line; a somewhat defeatist attitude but one which means that you will not find yourself badly out of position if the wind changes against you.

PRACTICAL NAVIGATION 91

NAVIGATION UNDER SAIL

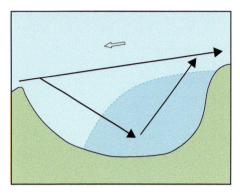

Deviating the course into a bay can have a number of benefits

along a coastline with a route set between headlands. Here there are several options.

7. Making a landfall

When making a landfall there are tactics that you can adopt to take advantage of expected wind shifts. We have already mentioned how the wind can veer as it moves from land to sea due to the difference in the friction between the surfaces over which the wind is flowing. Therefore, when approaching land, try to do so initially when on the starboard tack and then, as you find the wind veering on the approach to land, switch to the port tack so that you can take advantage of the wind shifting and can make a direct run in.

Expect changeable winds when sailing along a coastline with high cliffs

Tidal flow and apparent wind

Now we must look at the effects of the tide on your planning. To understand this complication you need to understand the meaning of 'apparent' wind. When a yacht is sailing ahead at a defined speed it meets a wind that is coming from a certain direction at another speed. This 'true' wind would be felt on board in the exact direction of the wind if the boat was stopped but because the boat is moving forward the speed and direction of the boat has to be combined with the speed and direction of the wind to find the apparent wind. The apparent wind is what the sails use to generate forward speed. The faster you go, the greater the benefit of the apparent wind, as demonstrated by the America's Cup catamarans that can sail faster than the true wind. They are able to do this because they are generating their own strong, apparent wind.

Tide can have an influence on the apparent wind. When the tide is with you, a two knot tide will logically add another two knots to your speed but it can also increase the angle and speed of the apparent wind, which can allow the speed to increase even more. With the tide against you, the apparent wind decreases its effect and you go relatively slower. This effect is not very noticeable on fast cruisers but on slow sailboats it can have a significant impact on performance. To make the most of it, plan your passage so as to have the tide with you on those parts of the passage where the tide flows most strongly, such as around headlands.

Lee-bowing is a further tidal effect which can impact upon apparent wind. It is most apparent in lighter winds and strong tides, when the wind and tide are at right angles to each other. In this scenario the tide pushes the boat towards the wind, this brings the apparent wind further aft and allows the boat to sail closer to the wind.

These are complex factors that can affect the performance of a sailboat. When making a passage they should be anticipated as far as possible so that their impact can be assessed

NAVIGATION UNDER SAIL

All the navigation information has to be squeezed onto a single display for most sailboat installations

in your mind and suitable allowances made. The ability to make such evaluations used to be an essential skill of a good sailor but electronic systems are also able to do many of the calculations for you.

Leeway

Information on leeway, the amount that the yacht is being set sideways by the pressure of the wind on the sails, must be obtained by 'intelligent guesswork'. Traditionally, it was estimated by looking over the stern and watching the wake. This would go off at a slight angle from the actual heading of the yacht and you could estimate the angle and allow for it. With experience, it is possible to forecast what the leeway will be by knowing your yacht, the strength of the forecast wind, and how you will be sailing. Leeway is likely to be at its highest when you are close-hauled but the type of keel on your yacht can also have an influence; a long straight keel probably offering less resistance to sideways movement than a deep, wide fin keel. You might want to allow a couple of degrees for leeway in lighter winds and increase this to perhaps 5° in a strong wind. The alternative is to make no allowance and to simply watch how the cross track error develops on the GPS plot before bringing the yacht back on track based on this.

It is not easy to differentiate between the effects of leeway and tide on the yacht, particularly if you are tacking into the tide or have the tide running with you. It does not really matter which effect is which. What is more important is the combined effect; this will be more or less the difference between the course and speed over the ground and the course and speed through the water, both of which can be measured.

The wind triangle

The wind triangle combines:

- the reading of the apparent wind angle
- the boat's course
- the boat's speed through the water.

These are all factors that can be measured on board. Apparent wind angle and speed can now be measured by the familiar masthead sensors, their cups measuring the speed, and the vane displaying the direction. As you sail along, you will notice that these elements vary due to the heeling of the boat as it passes over waves and the masthead moves at varying speeds. On more sophisticated systems, these movements are averaged out to provide a more reliable reading and the sensors are moved as far away from the mast as is practical to reduce any influence of the wind around the mast and sail. These readings are then combined with the boat speed and course through the water so that the wind triangle can be computed.

Note that it is course and speed through the water that is used and from this information the apparent wind speed and direction can be deduced and compared with the heading so that the best course for close-hauled sailing can be shown. You will also want to know the true wind direction so that

Masthead sensors for wind direction and speed

you can detect any wind shifts; this is calculated from the true wind angle and the compass heading data.

Angles and directions

It is worth noting here that when talking about instruments and sailing in general any value relative to the boat is referred to as an angle, whilst any value that is relative to an external point, is referred to as a direction.

You assess the wind in terms of the direction that it is coming from, i.e. a northerly wind comes from the north, whereas a heading is seen as the direction that you are moving towards i.e. if you are heading east then you are moving towards the east.

If you keep this in mind you should be able to get a clear picture of what all the directions and angles mean but remember that not all equipment manufacturers use this logical terminology. As far as the course and heading are concerned, a heading is what the compass is showing whilst the course is the direction of the boat through the water.

To arrive at the course you need to make an addition or subtraction for the leeway. Leeway is normally anything between 1° and 5° and you can get instruments that will calculate the leeway and apply it automatically.

With sailing instruments the compass and log readings should not be confused with the speed and course over the ground (SOG and COG) which are obtained from the GPS readings and shown on the plotter.

It is a complicated area but for sailing efficiency everything relates to the boat travelling through the water rather than the progress over the ground, which is a navigation computation. On a fast boat the effect of the tide will be much reduced because there is such a large difference between the boat's speed and the tide speed but on slow sailboats, the difference between the tide and the boat's speed can be quite small, so the effect of the tide is proportionally larger. This difference could make a considerable difference in the sailing information displayed.

A radar display on a cockpit display screen

NAVIGATION UNDER SAIL

Comprehensive electronic cockpit units are becoming more common

Velocity Made Good

What you are really interested in from the electronic instruments is the Velocity Made Good (VMG); the component of the boat speed that is made good in the direction of the wind.

When close-hauled, you want this figure to be as high as possible and you can adjust your heading to maximise this.

Beware that you might see some short term gains in VMG if you head up slightly into the wind but it will drop back again because the sails will pick up performance as you round slightly into the wind and then drop off. Obviously the VMG will be zero when the wind is abeam, if it isn't, your instruments need checking! The VMG can be used as a yardstick for sail efficiency and you may sometimes find that it increases if you ease the sails a touch, even though there may be little change in the boat speed.

Lay lines

A lay line is the ground track that the boat needs to follow in order to make the next waypoint or turning mark. When you are tacking towards a waypoint the lay line should indicate the moment at which to tack in order to make the waypoint. For maximum efficiency you should never cross a lay line but tack in order to sail along it.

Experienced sailors will be able to judge when to turn onto a lay line, it is part of the skill of sailing, but it can become complicated when you have a strong tide.

The tidal flow will have a considerable impact on the direction of the lay line so you need to make judgements about this. Setting a course along a lay line is fine provided that the wind and tide remain constant but this is rarely the case and if the turning mark or waypoint is off a headland you can often find the wind veering or backing as you approach the headland and the tide increasing in strength. On a cruising yacht you will, therefore, want to make generous allowances for possible changes in the wind and tide, unless you want to find yourself tacking right up to the waypoint. When racing, fine judgements about the lay line setting must be made in order to not lose time tacking.

Summary

It is clear that when navigating a sailboat there are many factors to consider. If you sail by the seat of your pants you will probably be able to make good progress but you will no doubt be less efficient than someone who has used all available information to take the best route possible in the conditions. Electronic instruments can be a considerable aid in helping to assess many of the variable factors but at the current stage of development they can never tell the full story, so experience and instinct are still valuable tools when navigating under sail.

PRACTICAL NAVIGATION

9 Navigation under power

On the face of it, navigating under power seems quite straightforward. You simply sort out the waypoints that you want to follow and then proceed along the route that you have planned. You could even get the chart plotter to set the route for you if it has auto-route facilities. You are not constrained by the direction of the wind and if the boat wanders a bit off course you simply alter it by a few degrees on the autopilot to correct things. In fact, you can even set the electronics for this to be applied automatically. Then, in fine weather, you can sit back, relax and almost let the boat take charge.

However, once at sea nothing is quite as it seems, conditions change rapidly and if you relax too much events can have a habit of taking over.

Use caution when navigating under power

If you think that you might be able to just sit back and relax, it may suggest that you are not keeping the level of lookout that the conditions demand.

You may not be checking out the position and course as you should be in order to ensure that the electronics are doing their job. You might have set alarms to give what you think is adequate warning of approaching dangers. Your concentration levels, therefore, drop to the point where if there is a problem or warning, it could take you some time to respond. On a fast motor cruiser you may be travelling at 25–30 knots, which is close to a mile every two minutes, and at that speed a lot can happen in a short time. You may have the navigation fully under control but how good is your lookout? Will you spot a floating object in the water far enough ahead to take avoidance action? Are you likely to see the approaching wash of another vessel that could take you and your crew by surprise if you don't slow down before you encounter it? Remember that even when the horizon looks clear and inviting there is always the possibility of something happening at short notice.

Fishing marks can be a hazard for motorboats and can only be reliably detected by a visual lookout

Wheelhouse design can compromise the ability to keep a good visual lookout

Visual navigation is the only reliable solution for narrow channels like this

96 PRACTICAL NAVIGATION

NAVIGATION UNDER POWER

Clear channel markers make navigation easy here

Making a comfortable journey

On a motor cruiser you are free to follow your desired course, with no constraints from the wind direction but it might still be worth thinking about alternative courses. On many voyages you will be faced with lively sea conditions. Alternative courses may give you a smoother ride and make life on board more comfortable.

Altering your speed

So concentration is still key when you are navigating a motor cruiser or powerboat but when you are navigating the boat from inside a wheelhouse this is not always as easy as it sounds. The fact that you are inside means that the outside world tends to become rather distant and you will find that your concentration tends to focus on the electronic displays rather than what is going on outside. Visibility from inside a wheelhouse on many boats is not always as good as it should be and it is surprising how many have no view astern from the helm. Saltwater smearing on the windscreen can reduce visibility and at night you cannot always be aware of where the blind spots might be. You probably can't do much to change things in the short term but at least if you are aware of the limitations of what you can see beyond the wheelhouse you might be able to take steps to mitigate these limitations.

Motor cruisers tend to have an uncomfortable motion when they are pitching into head seas because of the speed of encounter between waves. The boat does not often have time to recover from one wave before encountering the next one and so everybody on board can face a very uncomfortable ride that quickly dispels the enjoyment of the cruise. The most obvious solution is to slow down but this does not always produce the desired effect and can simply prolong the agony. In a head sea a planing boat will tend to span the wave crests, keeping a more or less level ride between them. This works well until the waves reach a certain critical size, at which point the bow might start to drop between wave crests and you can find yourself pitching and slamming into the waves in a very uncomfortable way. You slow down but can then find that the hull starts to contour the wave, with the pitching motion increasing even though the boat is going slower. You try to find the speed that is the most comfortable for the circumstances but

Passing close to a buoy gives a good navigation fix

PRACTICAL NAVIGATION 97

NAVIGATION UNDER POWER

Local knowledge would be helpful navigating round these rocks

Fast boat navigation requires a high level of concentration

the cruise can quickly switch from an enjoyable experience to one that you long to end.

This scenario is one that you could easily face if the wind proves stronger than forecast or if you find yourself dealing with the aftermath of swell of a passing storm. There is also always the risk that the waves that you encounter out at sea are larger than the forecast suggested. If you find that you have to slow down, this can make a significant difference to your ETA, especially with a planing boat where you may have to make a significant reduction in speed to get a comfortable ride. With a slower displacement boat the speed reduction is likely to be considerably less, you may even find that your do not need to reduce you speed at all. However, with both types of boat it is worth looking at tactics to improve your cruise.

Altering your course

An alteration in course can be a good solution, particularly if you are facing head seas. A small alteration could make a significant difference to your passage and save you from battling against the seas. When you put the seas on the bow rather than directly ahead you are effectively increasing the wave length so that the speed of encounter with the waves will be reduced; this can make quite a difference to ride comfort. Even an alteration of 20° can be enough to improve things and will only make a small difference to the distance you need to cover.

With the waves on the beam you should not have too many problems unless there has been a significant increase in wave height but in a displacement boat in beam seas you might want to make a small alteration up into the wind to help reduce the rolling. You may also find that the boat is making leeway in a beam wind and sea, i.e. being set downwind slightly by the pressure of the wind on the side of the hull. Your plot should show this as cross track error that can be corrected by altering course a few degrees up into the wind.

Leeway is unlikely to be more than a couple of degrees and you are most likely to experience this on an open sea passage. In following seas it might help to experiment with small alterations of course and see how the ride comfort changes, particularly with slower displacement boats. It is also possible

NAVIGATION UNDER POWER

Lively seas can make it harder to detect navigation marks

to try different flap settings but this is moving away from the navigational side of cruising.

Small changes of course can bring significant benefits when navigating planing hulls and it is definitely worth experimenting with changes in both speed and course. Look at your options for seeking out areas of more sheltered waters, for example, heading into bays when there is a head wind. This may add a bit more distance to your journey but there can be benefits. Firstly, by heading into the bay, you will be putting the sea on the bow and thus effectively increasing the distance between wave crests, this should give you an improved ride. Then, as you come under the shelter of the land on your approach to the next headland, the waves will be considerably reduced and you will be able to maintain good progress. Of course you will still have to negotiate your way around the headland itself as you come out of the shelter but at least you will have had some respite in the meantime.

Headlands and tidal flow

Headlands can present a challenge for any coastal passage because not only can the wind strength be increased temporarily but there can also be a stronger tidal flow. Tidal flow can be important when navigating a fast motor cruiser not so much because of the effect on speed but because it can have a considerable impact on the waves. When the wind and tide are flowing in the same direction the wave length is increased, effectively meaning that the waves are less steep, which can lead to a more comfortable ride. When the wind is against the tide the wave length is reduced and you can face more challenging sea conditions that may necessitate a reduction in speed. This often occurs off headlands, where the tidal flow is increased and there may be a noticeable tidal race with steep breaking waves at certain stages of the tide. You might want to try to plan your passage past a headland to coincide with slack water in order to get a smoother ride but the chances of being able to get it right at every headland on a coastal passage are not high as you only have the tide in your favour for approximately six hours out of twelve.

When navigating a coastal passage in fresh wind, the tide continues to be an important factor. You will need to consider the headland and its underwater contours carefully in order to be able to anticipate the conditions and the best distance off for the passage past. You can make a relatively smooth passage by passing just a short distance off some headlands, where the ideal flow can be very much reduced. This requires deep water close inshore and no off-lying rocks or shallows extending out from the headland. The areas of breaking waves can be extended offshore if there are shallows extending out from the headland. These may be deep enough for you to navigate across but the tidal flow across the

Challenging sea conditions can be found off many headlands

NAVIGATION UNDER POWER

A headland can provide a good steering mark

shallows can expand the area of breaking waves. Each headland has its own characteristics and whilst the main areas of a tide race will generally be marked on the chart you will need to make a judgement about how far off this is likely to extend, depending on the prevailing conditions at the time. You don't want to pass too far off the headland and extend the distance that has to be travelled but if you are too close in the conditions could be very challenging, although potentially quite short-lived.

In slower displacement motorboats, headlands can be equally challenging areas to navigate in, principally because you will take longer to pass through the area.

At slower speeds the tides will also have a much stronger influence on your speed over the ground. At 25 knots a two knot tide is not going to make a huge difference to your average speed but at six knots the difference can be considerable with the speed against

The electronic display can be much more interesting than the outside view

Calculating your fuel consumption

Finding out just what your consumption is, is not always easy, even though most engines now show the fuel consumption on the engine monitoring display. Here the consumption is usually shown in litres per hour which is not a very helpful figure. What you need to know is the fuel consumption per mile, which relates the fuel consumed to the actual distance covered, just as we find in cars. Some engine displays will show this when there is a GPS speed input added to the equation but you have to do the sums manually.

It is not difficult to do this; just divide the litres per hour figure by the speed, i.e. the miles per hour, this will give you the number of litres used for every mile covered. The speed used should be the speed over the ground, which will include any tidal influence. This is the figure you need in order to find out if the boat is running at an economical speed.

the tide being perhaps half that which you experience when the tide is running with you.

You should plan your passage to exploit favourable tides but when the tide is against you, deviating into a bay where there will be less tide can have a considerable influence on your passage time and more than make up for the additional distance steamed. Whilst the tide can have a considerable influence on the speed of slower boats, the need to slow down because of adverse sea conditions can often be less and you may only need to knock a knot or two off your normal speed. Adverse conditions may, therefore, have less impact on the time required to complete a passage than if you were in a planing boat.

Fuel consumption

Part of your passage planning, of course, involves ensuring that you have enough fuel on board to complete the passage and an adequate reserve. It makes sense not to cut things too fine and to have more than adequate fuel.

In most cases, slowing down due to the prevailing conditions should reduce your fuel consumption, particularly in a displacement boat. In a planing boat the fuel

NAVIGATION UNDER POWER

consumption should also decrease with a reduction in speed but if you have to come down off the plane, your consumption per mile could increase. The same applies if you have to operate on just one engine for any reason. Eventualities of this nature must be taken into account.

You will also find that fuel consumption increases as you motor into a head wind and sea, because of the increased resistance.

It can be useful to make a table showing what the consumption is at various speeds so that you can establish what the change in consumption will be if you have to change speed during a passage.

A good consumption table should also include information on consumption at slow displacement speeds on a planing boat and consumption when running on one engine. Both of these scenarios could lead to an increase in consumption per mile which you might like to factor in when planning the fuel requirements for your voyage. Any

A small box on this monitoring unit gives the fuel consumption in litres per mile

Filling up is a good chance to assess the fuel situation

It is best not to pass too close to beacons as they stand on the shoal or rock they are marking

consumption table showing the consumption per mile will have been developed for running when there is no tidal influence so to evaluate the actual consumption you need to take into account the change in speed under the influence of the tide.

Bear in mind that consumption will increase with adverse winds and waves but you are not likely to get a corresponding benefit when running with a following wind and sea. Also bear in mind that such a table will only be valid when there is no tidal influence, obviously when the tide is in your favour you will cover more miles per litre than when the tide is against you.

Summary

Navigating under power looks straightforward and in most situations it is. In good cruising conditions there are few, if any, restrictions on where you go as long as there is adequate water depth.

When you are faced with adverse conditions such as a freshening wind or when sea conditions are affected by the tides you are entering a changing scenario where you may need to consider alternative strategies to make life more comfortable and enjoyable on board and to make good progress against the flow.

It is clear that passage planning is an important tool even when undertaking what looks like a straightforward voyage in a motor boat, keep an open mind and be prepared to change your plans.

10 Coping with electronic failure

When I first started boating, it was normal to distrust anything electrical on a boat and it was considered quite a bonus if anything on board that was powered by electricity was actually working.

Your navigation tended, therefore, to focus on using a compass, a watch, and visual navigation. It was widely maintained that electricity and water should not mix and that when they did it was the water that always won.

Dramatic improvements in onboard electrical systems mean that such ideas are largely a thing of the past and nowadays we rely on electrical power for virtually every element of a voyage.

Electronic systems are the core of modern navigation and most solid-state electronics are incredibly reliable. They are no longer sensitive to the pounding and motions of a boat at sea in rough weather and they are fully watertight, meaning they can even be installed in open positions in the cockpit. So you might well ask, why not depend on the electronics entirely for navigation? The answer is that electronics can and do fail and it is vital to know how to cope if you find yourself in this situation.

Electrical supply

There can be various reasons for electrical issues on board; the first thing to consider would be a failure in the electrical supply to the units. If all the electronic navigation systems go down, then this will almost certainly be the cause and it may just be a case of re-setting the breaker that controls those circuits or replacing the fuse on older boats.

Modern boats usually have separate breakers for each individual electronic item. For example, there may be one breaker for the radar and one for the chart plotter although smaller items such as the sounder and the log may be put on the one common breaker. If any one unit goes down, the first step is to check the appropriate breaker and reset it if possible. If you can reset it and it stays in then it is probably just a one-off occurrence but if you can't reset it and it wants to stay open, it is possible that there may be a fault in the wiring that supplies the power in that circuit.

This may not be easily fixed at sea because the dashboard will have to be dismantled in order to get to the wiring behind and you will need to cope without that unit. In this situation, having each unit

Melted insulation in hidden areas is what can cause an electrical failure for the electronics

The electric wiring on some boats is not up to the highest standards

on a separate breaker is a clear advantage, as you will only lose one unit if there is a power supply failure of this type. There is complex wiring behind most dashboards these days and often it is a case of out of sight, out of mind.

Wiring is not always installed to the highest standards, so chafing of the wires or loose or corroded connections are always a possibility. The best you can do to anticipate a failure of this type is to make yourself familiar with which breaker controls what and to check where they are located so you can find them quickly in the middle of the night. Understanding how the electrical system works can go some way towards helping you to cope with an electrical fault when you are out at sea.

Electronic failure

Unfortunately, if the radar fails there is little that can be done because there is no real back-up system. Checking the electrical supply is about as much as you can do. A failure with the chart plotter, meanwhile, is easily resolved by having a portable, handheld plotter on board. These operate from a battery power supply, which makes them a great back up. Of course you will need to have a suitable chart cartridge fitted if you want to get the full plotting function but even without that you can still get a GPS position from the unit and enter waypoints to obtain a course. These can be used as they stand or they can be plotted on a paper chart to get you home. If you want a really useful back up service from your handheld chart plotter, you should enter the matching waypoints from your main system into the handheld unit. You can then get course, speed and cross track error readings even without a chart cartridge. However, you will probably not want to go this far in terms of back up and a much better solution would be to have both your main plotter and the handheld using compatible chart cartridges. If you are running a motor cruiser, do remember that the handheld GPS receiver may not work inside the wheelhouse because the GPS antenna incorporated into the unit may not be able to receive the GPS signal from inside the boat. Nowadays, a mobile phone can also provide many of the same features as a portable plotter, provided you have a suitable chart app installed. You can still get a GPS position without an app but, again, you are unlikely to pick up a GPS signal inside the wheelhouse.

GPS failure

In my experience, an electrical failure is now a rare event because the standard of installation has improved considerably. GPS failure is likely to cause much more concern. I have already discussed the fragility of the GPS signal and to me it remains a wonder that despite the weak signals, GPS remains very reliable.

However, the signal has been known to go down. There can be several reasons for this.

- Firstly, there is the possibility of a satellite failure, which, although rare, does happen. The Russian equivalent to GPS, the Glonass system, went down for half a day recently.

A handheld chart plotter with its own GPS can be a good stand-by

COPING WITH ELECTRONIC FAILURE

- You can check whether the system is operational by going to the satellite page on the plotter and seeing which satellites are being received or you can check if your handheld unit is still receiving signals. If it is, then it is your GPS antenna or the chart plotter that is at fault.

- If the GPS system itself is at fault, it is likely to be a temporary glitch and there is nothing you can do except wait for it to come back online again.

GPS jamming

Other potential causes of a GPS failure are jamming and spoofing. This is discussed in detail in Chapter 2.

Jamming

Jamming is when someone sets off a powerful signal at or near the same frequency of the GPS signal, thereby drowning it out. However, even if jamming did occur, not all would be lost. Because GPS is a military system and a failure could have serious consequences, research has been carried out to develop anti-jamming antennas that can be incorporated into GPS receivers. Sensitive filters that can sense and separate the jamming signal from the GPS signal are built into the antenna.

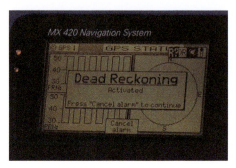

On this unit, dead-reckoning is activated if the GPS fails

We are starting to see some of this technology being incorporated into the high-end antennas of commercial GPS receivers, which is one reason for not opting for one of the cheap receivers available on the market. The GPS antenna in your mobile phone is likely to be at the cheap end of the range, whilst that of a dedicated marine receiver should be higher quality.

Miniature filter systems are also now available on the commercial market. These claim to reduce the impact of jamming signals and can be incorporated into the GPS antenna link. They are based on the military technology and may become familiar in the future. Technology is constantly evolving but it is a challenging situation.

Spoofing

Spoofing is potentially a much more serious problem for boats. With spoofing, a rogue transmitter not only sends out a signal that overrides the GPS signal but also modifies it in such a way that the GPS still works but shows a false position. This could lead to serious navigational mistakes.

However, if you are closely monitoring your position and the plotted course, you should notice any sudden jump to a new position.

If this happens, make a note of the last 'real position' and then try to fix your position visually or by radar. The GPS alarm may go off when spoofing occurs but there is no guarantee, particularly if the change in position is quite small.

This GPS antenna has been repaired with tape - not a good sign for reliability

104 PRACTICAL NAVIGATION

COPING WITH ELECTRONIC FAILURE

Other transmitters

Finally, GPS can be affected by powerful transmitters in the vicinity of your boat. These do not have to be on the same frequency as the GPS, their sheer power may be enough to overwhelm the GPS frequency and signal. I have only come across one example of this, in the waters near Portofino in northern Italy. Here there is a powerful aircraft beacon on the headland that acts as a guide for aircraft coming in to land at nearby Genoa airport. You can lose the GPS signal anywhere within an approximate three mile radius of this beacon.

In the US, meanwhile, where a loss of GPS signal was noticed within a mile of one particular marina, the fault was traced to a powerful pre-amplifier on board one of the moored yachts. Any powerful transmitter of this type that affects your GPS is likely to be on shore which means interference will occur at a time when, close to shore, you may be placing a heavy reliance on GPS positioning.

Alarms

It is likely, therefore, that you will be relying on GPS for most of your navigation, so it is important to consider what to do if the GPS failure alarm comes up on the screen. If the GPS goes down for any reason you will probably get warnings from several sources. With modern integrated electronic systems the GPS will definitely be fed into the chart plotter, and the AIS if you have it, but it could also be used by the radar, the autopilot and even possibly by the VHF radio, where it can send the position if it is coupled with an automatic distress call system. All of these are likely to sound or show an alarm to warn of the problem and you are likely to spend the first few minutes of GPS signal loss trying to sort out the alarms rather than doing anything about the loss of position.

The first thing to do once the alarms have been silenced is to make a note of the time and coordinates of the last position shown on the plotter, plus the course being steered. Of course, in an ideal world you should have been keeping a logbook record of positions and courses every half an hour, or more frequently on a faster boat. Every boat should have a logbook, it not only provides a record of what you have done and where you have been over the years but can be a useful font of information if you do find yourself with an electronic or GPS failure.

Each time you leave harbour you should record the time of departure, the heading, the weather conditions and any other relevant information. You will probably know your departure point outside the harbour by reference to a navigation buoy or mark but it is a good discipline to write down your latitude and longitude positions every half an hour or so, in order to have a reference point from which to navigate if the electronic positions fail.

Relying solely on GPS in inshore waters can be a recipe for disaster

PRACTICAL NAVIGATION 105

COPING WITH ELECTRONIC FAILURE

If you are a serious navigator, you will also be keeping a separate plot of the course on a paper chart and making checks using the visual clues along the track that we talked about earlier in the book. This means that if your GPS or electronic chart system goes down, you will still know where you are and where to go. However, it is very easy to bypass this precaution and ninety nine percent of the time you are likely to get away with it. The excellent reliability of electronics is both a blessing and a curse as on the rare occasions that it does go wrong you tend to not have taken precautions against it.

It you stop receiving positions from the GPS, some electronic chart systems will continue to plot the track using dead reckoning based on the last course and speed that were being used. This should at least get you to somewhere near your destination or next waypoint at which point visual navigation can take over but you will not get any cross track error. In this situation it is important to maintain the same course and speed. The possibility of electronic failure is one good reason to set the autopilot manually rather than integrate it directly with the chart system. At least you will then have the course to steer. If your autopilot goes down along with the rest of the system,

eLoran

Because GPS is now such an important source of both position and time information for so many people, studies are being made to find an alternative. eLoran is the frontrunner; it is a robust, terrestrial-based system whose powerful transmitters are much more difficult to jam. eLoran receivers have been developed that said to give positional accuracy close to that of GPS and certainly accurate enough for general navigation. The system is already established for some local areas along the UK coast, with one covering the busy Dover Strait area.

Dual GPS and eLoran receivers are available today but with the limited coverage of eLoran at the time of writing it would be hard to justify the cost of such receivers on yachts and small craft.

Having two independent systems giving positions could also put you in a dilemma if they were showing different positions. Which one do you take as the correct position?

In time the system is likely to be expanded and the cost of suitable receivers should then fall but funding for eLoran is a political matter so expansion is not guaranteed. The 13-hour failure of the Russian Glonass system could very well focus attention towards funding for eLoran but nothing is certain as yet.

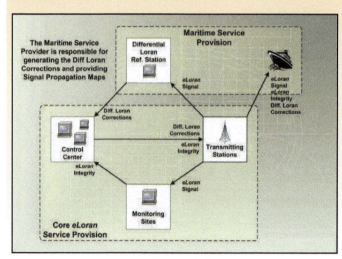

The operating system for an eLoran network

COPING WITH ELECTRONIC FAILURE

Keeping a log book is an important part of navigation

Two compass displays showing different readings!

you will have to resort to manual steering and navigation. This is when your magnetic compass comes into its own. It is the one navigation instrument that will keep working when everything else stops.

Using a compass

It is worth, therefore, considering the compass in more detail. With the electronics in full working order the compass has become almost redundant on small boats and I find that my use of it for navigation is much reduced these days. You tend to set the pre-ordained course on the autopilot and then nudge the heading a few degrees one way or the other when the chart plotter shows a cross track error developing.

To get the best from it, the compass display needs to be mounted where it can be seen and used and you will need access to the full 360° display.

Of course the magnetic compass, which one way or the other is at the heart of nearly every small boat compass, will show a compass heading rather than the true heading which would enable you to reference the course to the chart. Variation and deviation must be considered as part of what used to be the complex business of correcting a compass. The variation is pretty well fixed for the area you are sailing in and is a simple correction to apply, plus or minus according to whether it is east or west; on electronic compasses this can be applied as a permanent fixture whereas with a basic magnetic compass you will need to apply the variation manually.

Deviation is the variable effect produced by the magnetic influence of the boat. Rather than go through the complexity of having the compass 'swung' to establish what the deviation is, you should be able to get sufficient accuracy simply by comparing the steering compass readings with those from a hand bearing or remote compass held away from anything that might be magnetic. One of the problems with the simple magnetic compass is that these days it is often mounted in a position where it is surrounded by electronic instruments. This can result in considerable deviation errors, depending on which electrical equipment is switched on and working and makes getting a reliable magnetic heading difficult. The best solution when using the compass as a back up is probably to note the compass reading when you are first setting a course using the electronic systems. You will then have this available if there is a GPS failure but, as noted, the compass error may change if there is an electrical failure.

PRACTICAL NAVIGATION **107**

COPING WITH ELECTRONIC FAILURE

Applying corrections

Applying corrections to compasses can be a tedious job but the modern fluxgate magnetic compass can make life easier. On fluxgate and electric compasses you can usually make the variation a permanent correction and can correct deviation by simply turning the boat in a circle with the compass switched to the calibrate setting, deviation corrections will then be applied automatically. You will need to decide whether to operate the courses as true or compass courses. A fluxgate compass will still be influenced by any nearby magnetic material and as the sensors for these compasses are usually mounted somewhere inside the boat, make sure that nothing magnetic is stowed close by the compass unit.

GPS compasses

The GPS compass represents a new development in small boat compasses. It uses two GPS receivers located a fixed distance apart to produce readings that can be interpolated to measure the boat's heading as a digital readout. The heading display of the various electronic compasses can also vary a lot. They may only show the heading as a digital display, fine if you are steering on this but no use if you are trying to get rough relative bearings. I also find it hard to remember whether I should steer to port or starboard with one of these digital displays. Compass technology has come a long way and like most things related to navigation it has switched from simplicity to complex electronics but for me the full horizontal compass card display is still the best and represents another area where tradition can still offer the best and most reliable solution.

All this is deviating from the main subject of setting the course in case of electronic failure and there are good books that go into compasses in a lot more detail. My message is, don't ignore the compass. It can be a lifesaver if the electronics go down and I spent years going around the world with just a compass, watch and a sextant before electronic navigation came along. Call me old-fashioned but I love my compass!

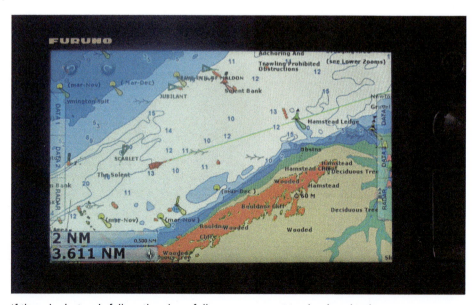

If there is electronic failure then hopefully you can revert to visual navigation

COPING WITH ELECTRONIC FAILURE

Chart system failure

Back to coping with electronic failure, if the chart system goes down either through an internal fault or an electrical failure, you still want to maintain the course and speed but you will need to pay more attention to possible visual clues. If you have a paper chart available it should not be too difficult to navigate to your destination. In a worst-case scenario, with no paper chart and no course, you should at least know the direction of the land from your passage planning work, so you can head in that direction and watch for visual clues. The depth sounder is vital here, and the risk of an electronic failure is a good reason for not having the sounder integrated into the chart system. If all else fails, you can always get direction clues from the wind and the sun, provided that you have been keeping note of these when the GPS was working. Many of the visual navigation techniques from this book should also help.

One way to give you more confidence in coping with electronic failure is to occasionally make a passage without the electronics switched on. Go back to basics using just the view out to the horizon, your compass and a watch and see how you get on. You will need to do a lot more planning beforehand to make this work but it will be a useful exercise and will hone your navigation skills.

Summary

You might think that I rather keep on about electronic failure, considering that in my experience it only happens very rarely but it is important to be prepared. The failure may be because the onboard electrical system has failed, it may be the GPS system going down or it could be an electronic failure in the equipment itself. Whatever and whenever it happens, I can assure you that you will feel bereft. You can suddenly feel very alone out at sea and having the course and position information written down will help to offer the reassurance that you need in this situation and, most importantly, it will enable you to find your way home.

PRACTICAL NAVIGATION *109*

11 Peripherals

The principal electronic navigation products for day-to-day sailing are the chart plotter and the radar.

They are the basics but there are a number of peripheral electronic navigation systems. Some of these, like the log and the sounder, can be integrated into the main electronics system or operate as independent units. Others, such as forward looking sonar and low light and thermal imaging cameras, may find their way into fully integrated systems in the future but at present tend to be standalone units.

The advent of reliable GPS positioning has changed the role of traditional standalone units such as the log and the sounder. Speed is now generally measured by interpreting sequential GPS positions. This gives the speed over the ground, which shows your progress towards the next waypoint and is, therefore, more useful for general navigation. However, speed over the ground gives no idea of the boat's performance when tidal streams enter the equation. Therefore, the independent log that measures speed through the water still has a place on most boats and is considered to be essential on sailboats, where being able to measure the speed through the water is vital when trimming the sails for performance.

Logs

All of these types of log should be calibrated if you want reliable results and there is usually a facility for this incorporated into the software of the units. The speed measured by the log can be displayed on a dashboard display or there is also a facility to convert the speed information into sailing performance units.

For these electronic logs to operate correctly, it is vital that the sensor units under the hull are kept clean and free from marine growth. Any barnacles or bits on the propeller or paddle wheel will reduce the accuracy of the readings and growth on electrical contacts will also reduce effectiveness. Relating the speed through the water to the speed over the ground can show you the effect of the tide.

By noting the differences in speed, log information can also tell you the sailing efficiency for different adjustments of the sails. The same technique can be used on a motor cruiser to show the effects of adjusting flaps or weight distribution.

Sounders

From a navigational point of view, the sounder is much more important.

Echo sounders were one of the original electronic systems, developed some 60 years

---

Logs

Speed log
The original speed log that works by towing a propeller through the water has now largely been replaced by an integral unit fitted to the hull. This may still have the carefully calibrated mini-propeller that measures the speed through the water by rotating at a speed directly related to the water flowing past. An alternative to the propeller is a paddle wheel.

Electronic log
A later version of the electronic log, meanwhile, has no moving parts at all and measures instead using two exposed contacts; the changing strength of the current flowing across the contacts is related to the speed of the boat.

Doppler
A more refined model of log is presented by the doppler, which finds the speed by measuring the change in frequency between the transmitted and received signals to calculate the velocity. This measures the speed through the water, although in shallow water it may also measure the speed over the ground.

PERIPHERALS

ago. The electronic systems give a continuous readout on a dashboard display but it is important to remember that the sounder only measures the depth under the boat and does not give any advance warning of approaching shallows, except by showing the trend of the sounders, where a steadily decreasing depth could indicate that there are shallows ahead. With this in mind, you are more likely to be interested in the trend of the measured depths, rather than the actual depth itself. This is why a display that shows the soundings over the past few minutes is more useful than a direct digital read out of the real time depth.

The sounder can also offer clues as to your position. When you look at the chart, your position must lie somewhere along the depth contour relating to the depth shown by the sounder, thereby enabling you to create a position line of sorts. A sudden steep change in depth will give a more precise position line than one where the depth is changing gradually but again this must be related to what you can see on the chart. The measurements from the sounder can, therefore, act as a useful check on the GPS plotting because the depth from the sounder should relate directly to the chart depth for the position shown, although you must of course bear in mind any tidal depth variations.

Transducers

Depth is measured from a transducer, which is normally mounted in the hull. This sends out a sound signal, which is then reflected back from the seabed. The depth is calculated by measuring the time that elapses between sending and receiving the signal, this is then halved.

For accurate readings, you need to know exactly where the depth reading is being measured from. If the transducer is located in the lowest part of the boat, which could be best if you are operating in shallow water, you will need to add the depth of the transducer from the surface plus any tidal variation in the depth to find the actual depth for a chart comparison.

On a sailboat the transducer will normally be hull mounted so you may have a few feet to take off to find the depth under the keel. It is important to know whether the reading has been adjusted to show the depth from the water surface or the depth under the keel. Most sounders allow for this adjustment but you can check which setting has been used on your sounder by measuring the actual depth from the surface using a weight on a rope and then relating this to the depth shown by the sounder. If the two correspond, the sounder is obviously set to measure the actual depth of water.

Displays

The depth measured by the sounder can be displayed in a number of ways. The simplest is a digital display that shows the current depth measured in either metres or feet, or perhaps on some older displays, in fathoms. You can get some idea of whether the depth

High quality echo sounders can provide a very clear picture of the sea bed

A dual display with the sounder and the chart on show

PRACTICAL NAVIGATION *111*

PERIPHERALS

A graphic sounder display can show trends as well as depth

Some of the peripherals available on modern electronic systems

of water is increasing or decreasing by seeing if the depth is going up or down, but it is much easier to see the trend if you have a graphic display that can be set to show the depth for the past few minutes or even further back. This can be valuable if you are making a landfall in reduced visibility or if you are crossing a shoal or trench and want to see where it begins and ends so that you have a sort of depth position line to confirm your position. This type of graphic display can often be shown on a split screen alongside the electronic chart and more sophisticated depth sounders also use this type of display when searching for fish. When you are using the sounder for navigation, remember that what you see displayed on the screen is essentially history as soon as you see it because it shows the depth directly under the boat and you will already have moved on by the time you read it.

With the advent of chart plotters there is less emphasis on the use of depth sounders but to my mind they still have a vital role to play in navigation. They are the 'eyes' underwater and provide a real time reading of the distance between you and the seabed. Without the sounder you have to rely on the depth information shown on the chart and this can be out of date and change with time. When there are differences between the sounder reading and your charted position, it can also provide an important warning that all is not well with the navigation.

Forward-looking sonar

An alternative type of sounder, with the capability to give some advance warning of danger, is the forward-looking sonar, the concept of which has been developed from the forward scanning sonars used by commercial fishermen to detect fish shoals. The sound signal is sent out ahead of the boat by a transducer mounted in the bow. This signal is reflected back from the seabed or any object ahead, so in theory you get a picture of what lies ahead underwater. The range of these forward looking sounders tends to be quite limited, perhaps just 200 metres ahead at best. The transducer for these sounds has to be underwater, which could be a problem when the boat is pitching in rough seas or on planing boats, where the bow lifts when the boat is on the plane.

There are two possible uses for forward-looking sonar as far as navigation is concerned.

A forward-looking sonar showing the weak returns from a mooring chain

112 PRACTICAL NAVIGATION

PERIPHERALS

- In the open sea it may be able to detect floating debris, such as a shipping container or tree trunk. Floating debris can be a major safety concern, particularly for fast boats, but the limited range of these sonars means there is some doubt as to whether you would detect anything in time to take avoiding action. With a closing speed of say 25 knots, you would only have a few seconds to take action and you would have had to be watching the display closely in the first place to spot the target ahead.

- The second possible use of forward-looking sonar would be when navigating a narrow channel. It should be possible to detect the sides of the channel and to gain a visual warning if you started to drift out of it.

These sonar sounders come in two types:

Two-dimensional display Gives a restricted picture of what lies ahead; features such as buoy chains and moorings do not show up very clearly and I would assume that any floating object might be equally hard to detect.

Three-dimensional display Gives a much clearer picture that is easier to understand; it

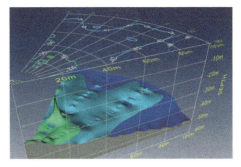

A 3D graphic display of the forward-looking sonar

is likely to be the best solution when navigating narrow channels. It is great to be able to see what lies ahead underwater and the sonar picture can be quite reassuring but any narrow channel in which you are navigating is likely to be marked to be marked by buoys or withies anyway so the forward looking sonar might seem to be a big investment for quite a small return.

Side-looking sonar

This sends out a sound signal from transducers on the side of the vessel to give you a picture of what is along each side. Like the echo sounder signal, these returns are

The shoaling ahead is visible on this forward-looking sonar display

PERIPHERALS

The camera unit for a low light camera with adjustable angle and azimuth

closer object. The potential for brighter lights to dominate the display can cancel out the camera's usefulness in harbours, an area where low light detection could be very helpful. Despite the Colregs, boats still operate without lights but you are not likely to pick these up with low light cameras when you have all the bright shore lights dominating the display. However, the quality of detection and the discrimination continue to improve with development.

The infrared camera works by picking up the slight differences in temperature between an object on the water and the water itself; this is magnified and displayed on a screen. This type of camera could be very useful in a man-overboard scenario at night, body heat allowing the camera to clearly highlight the person in the water. It could also be used when entering a small harbour at night, when there are no navigation lights. The infrared camera can detect very small differences in temperature and the returns can be enhanced by having an infrared searchlight fitted. This is shone ahead to help activate objects in your path. This would only work over a relatively short range but I have used the system at sea to pick up unlit fishing marks and it has worked well enough to allow a high speed to be maintained with a degree of confidence. Infrared cameras should still work in fog because the temperature differences will still be there, whereas the low light camera will be restricted in these conditions.

history by the time they are displayed but they could produce a check on your location in a narrow channel by highlighting the channel's edges. Again this type of sonar seems like a big investment for a fairly small return.

Low light and infrared cameras

The same argument could be used for the installation of low light and infrared cameras.

These are used to give an alternative view around the boat in difficult visibility conditions and are often confused with one another.

The low light camera enhances what little light there is to enable you to identify small targets that might otherwise be missed. The camera picks up small amounts of light emanating from other vessels or perhaps unlit buoys and magnifies it to make it stand out against the background. The display tends to be monochrome and the small light returns from some weak targets can be drowned out if there are any bright lights in the vicinity or in the distance beyond the

Both of these cameras add another layer of detection to the use of radar and visual observations. With the apparent increase in unlit objects and fishing markers floating out at sea, they do have the potential to be very useful, especially when navigating in inshore waters at night. However, in their present format their arc of detection can be quite limited and with some of the units you have to move the camera manually to scan the horizon. Infrared cameras have a limited range of probably around one mile but the low light cameras can pick up objects at a similar range to visual sightings. Low light and thermal cameras add yet another display

PERIPHERALS

A high quality low light camera display compared with the chart display above

screen to be monitored and do demand constant attention if you are going to detect an object in time to take avoidance action. This monitoring is likely to be at the expense of a visual lookout.

Both cameras come in two forms

- A fixed display screen linked to the external camera, which can be directed manually from a joystick control

- A handheld unit rather like binoculars.

Both types tend to offer a relatively narrow field of vision so you will need to focus on the display to get useful results, although there are low light cameras that can offer a wider field of vision and these could be useful when navigating in harbour.

The use of these cameras would be extended considerably if they carried out surveillance in much the same way as radar with a rotating camera. It would help detection if the camera and the radar were operating in sequence so that an object detected on the radar could then be viewed by a camera.

As we place more and more reliance on radar detection of targets, this type of integrated surveillance will be developed to the point where it becomes viable but you will still be left with the dilemma of where to concentrate your lookout.

Do you give preference to the electronic systems or to the manual lookout? Unfortunately there is no single system guaranteed to detect everything that is out there floating on the water and even when a number of systems are used in combination there are still no guarantees. The Colregs make no direct mention of these camera systems, although you could see camera use as an element of the previously discussed requirement to keep a lookout 'by all means possible'.

Heading information

This is a vital part of navigation in small craft and when it comes to compasses we tend to mainly talk about the basic magnetic compass. This is fitted as standard on boats of all shapes and sizes. It is self-contained and it does not require a power supply (except of course for a light when fitted) and it is virtually 100% reliable. We have already talked about alternative compass systems, such as the fluxgate compass, and their use is now widespread but there is still a place on board for the basic magnetic compass.

Fluxgate compass

Most autopilots use a modified fluxgate compass; a magnetic compass that senses the direction via a series of coils detecting the varying magnetic fields. This type of compass is often modified with the addition of a rate gyro, which helps the units to keep up when the boat is turning. Although it is still magnetic, it works well thanks to an incorporated self-calibration system that allows you to correct for deviations created by local magnetic influences on board.

These fluxgate compasses may eventually be superseded by GPS compasses. At one time the latter were an expensive luxury only used on ships. Now, their price has gone

PERIPHERALS

A traditional magnetic compass that needs no outside connections

The antenna for a GPS compass

down considerably and they are more compact. The GPS compass consists of two GPS receivers mounted a fixed distance apart in the same unit; the heading of the vessel is found by interpolating the difference between the two GPS receiver readings. The big benefit is that they give a true heading rather than a magnetic one. This means that there is no need to apply corrections, although there is always a slight delay in the heading reading out when the course is changing.

Aside from showing the course that you are steering, the magnetic compass can be quite useful for spatial orientation, getting a feel for what is happening around you and thinking about directions, particularly in collision avoidance situations. However, for this you need a compass display that presents the full 360° picture at a glance. Many compass displays only show a small section of the compass rose, perhaps just the bit that is currently relevant to steering the boat.

On some the heading is just a digital display, which may be fine as an autopilot reference but is not much use for manual steering or as a spatial reference.

Gyro and GPS compasses

There are two alternatives to the fluxgate compass. One is the gyro-compass, which has been around for a long time. In its early form, this was a highly complex and expensive piece of equipment that ruled it out for small craft use.

Today the gyro compass design has been refined and has reduced both in size and price, so that it has become a viable heading reference for smaller craft, although it still remains relatively expensive.

The advantage of the gyro-compass is that it gives a true heading because it does not rely in any way on magnetic readings.

The same can be said for the GPS compass. Usually the two GPS antenna required for this compass are mounted in a single unit about a metre long and the positions will, again, be a true heading. Because the two GPS receivers are picking up virtually the same signal, any errors in the GPS positioning is taken out of the equation because the positions are compared rather than used in absolute form. These compasses can produce a heading with an accuracy of around one tenth of a degree but until recently they have been too expensive for general small boat use. Both the size and the cost are coming down, although this is at the expense of the accuracy. The price is now within an acceptable level for small craft use, as is the size, and the accuracy of these new units is in the order of 2°, which, again, is acceptable for small craft use.

Accelerometers

Another innovation is the use of accelerometers and gyros in a package that can give you a short-term inertial navigation system. By simply sensing the movement of the boat, these units can give a remarkably accurate dead-reckoning system without the need for any outside links or connections. They are similar to the highly complex

PERIPHERALS

Virtually every yacht has masthead sensors these days

systems that used to be fitted on aircraft and nuclear submarines and they offer the prospect of a fully independent back-up navigation system that does not require any outside reference. However, at the present stage of development, they are not widely available or in use, except for specialised applications.

Offshore weather information

Before you head out to sea you will have looked at the latest weather information on the internet and listened to radio forecasts, but once away from the shore you are likely to lose your internet connection unless you have expensive satellite links. You may be on your own as far as updated weather information is concerned, unless you have satellite phone coverage or an SSB radio enabling you to pick up GRIB weather information. Some of the more sophisticated electronic systems can offer an overlay of a weather map. This can be vital if you are on a longer cruise, say across the Bay of Biscay, but you usually have to pay for this level of up-to-date weather information.

Any weather information that you are able to obtain when you are offshore is likely to be rather general in nature and not the sort of detailed information, such as wind shifts and, of course, the development of stronger winds, that you really need. Ocean weather maps will show the general trend of the weather patterns but you will also have to rely on your own interpretations of what you can see outside and what the verbal radio forecasts are saying. The wave heights that are given by these forecasts will be average heights and should only be relied on as an indication of what to expect rather than as specific forecasts. Good quality forecasts out at sea are probably the one major weakness of the modern electronic system and if you want this information, you will need to invest in some means of getting internet coverage from satellite links. Weather is now becoming an integral part of navigation at sea and for coastal navigation the availability of good quality information should be an important consideration. You may want to navigate to maintain land contact as much as possible so as to benefit from the mobile phone and internet coverage that it provides.

Summary

The peripheral devices covered in this chapter tend to get overshadowed by the advances in radar and electronic charts but simple systems such as the log and compass do provide the independent back that can be useful when you have electronic failures of one sort or another. These basic systems are also being incorporated into the mainstream instruments, so they could well lose their independence in the future. The more complex peripherals may well find their way into the mainstream with development but at present there is a question mark over what they offer in terms of value for money and their potential to distract you from the main navigation focus.

PRACTICAL NAVIGATION *117*

12 Phones, tablets and computers

The introduction of computers onto boats has been a slow process and in the past it was only the brave who took their laptops to sea as an aid to navigation and communication. Desktop computers have never really found their way onto yachts, with the exception of superyachts, because of their size, sensitivity to bumps and bangs, and the difficulty of organising the required power supplies. Even laptops were vulnerable in the harsh sea-going environment and tended to be used reluctantly. The introduction of the tough, modern laptop changed things considerably, bringing with it an influx of software that could help the navigator. The new laptop was less power hungry, although you still needed a mains power supply for the charger, and its compact size and prolonged battery life made it a much more viable unit for use on board. A large number of boaters now take their laptops to sea, although in many cases this is for internet access rather than to assist with navigation.

Background

When using a laptop for navigation, there was always the issue of getting a GPS feed into the computer to give you position information and a CD drive tended to be necessary. Today there are a number of USB dongles that can do the job.

To protect the laptop from excess movement and to keep it dry, it had to be located inside the boat, which wasn't necessarily the most convenient location for navigation, particularly on a sailboat, nor the best spot for picking up GPS signals from the dongle.

The navigation laptop came onto the scene at about the same time that GPS was becoming firmly established, and it competed with the chart plotters from the established marine manufacturers.

The laptop offered a relatively cheap and flexible approach to electronic navigation in the form of a chart plotter.

The dedicated electronic navigation systems were more expensive but in their various forms they offered the full suite of navigation displays.

The laptop could not provide radar or an echo sounder so its navigation use was

Weather charts from the Internet displayed on a laptop

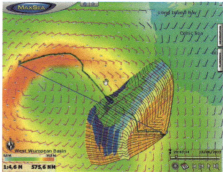

Weather routing information displayed in relation to the forecast winds

PHONES, TABLETS AND COMPUTERS

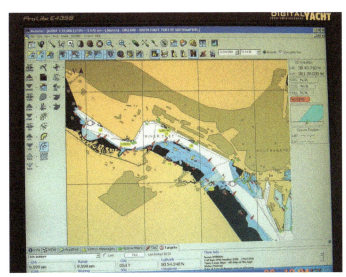

Chart systems designed for computers tend to have a large range of icons, which can be confusing on a small screen

limited but it could, of course, be used for normal computer operations such as internet access and word processing. The laptop was a cheaper solution, but it was not waterproof, nor was it designed for the often harsh environment of a boat. Its use was very much a matter of personal preference and budget and a few years ago you saw a laptop on virtually every boat of significant size. You still see them fairly frequently now but their role has changed from that of a navigation tool to a means of personal communication and they are generally packed away when the boat goes to sea as they lose their connection to the internet.

Passage planning software

There is specialist software available that is more applicable to passage planning than to real time navigation and this can be very valuable to those who want to plan their passage in the comfort of their own home.

The software can be programmed with tidal information, so it automatically applies tidal flow corrections to a planned course.

You can also display the forecast winds, which have been picked up from the internet, nearer the time of departure so that your possible routes plotted on the software can be made wind sensitive. The running of this software is perhaps the principal role of the laptop in future navigation.

Laptops at sea

The use of laptop software at sea can be more limited because the icons used on the display are often quite small and difficult to pick out and using the touch pad and keyboard is not particularly easy on a boat that is moving about at sea.

You also have to secure the laptop somehow, so that it does not come adrift if the boat rolls heavily. Power supply for the laptop can be arranged with the use of inverters that raise the boat's voltage to that of mains supplies for the charger.

These comments also apply to the smaller netbooks but the major cause of both laptops and netbooks taking a back seat, as

Using a laptop for navigation at sea

PRACTICAL NAVIGATION 119

PHONES, TABLETS AND COMPUTERS

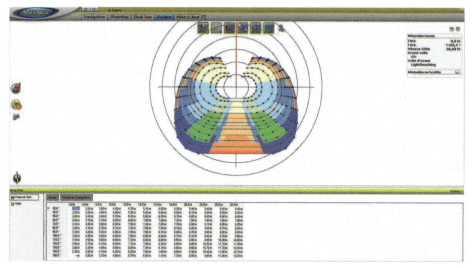

A polar diagram on a computer that can be integrated into a performance prediction programme

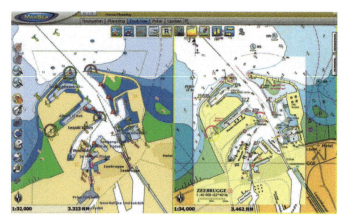

Some computer programmes can show vector and raster versions of the same chart alongside each other

far as navigation is concerned, has been the introduction of the smartphone and, subsequently, the tablet or pad.

Smartphones

The ubiquitous smartphone, including the iPhone, was first introduced as an upmarket mobile phone and much of what it does is related to land-based requirements.

However, it has become a wonderful navigation device for use at sea. To use it well, it is important that you narrow down exactly what you want it to do rather than allowing yourself to be overwhelmed by the wide variety of apps on offer.

The smartphone, together with the relevant apps, is the most complete navigation tool ever invented. In one tiny handheld unit it can offer communication, navigation, charting and positioning, a compass, tides and currents, AIS, and even a logbook, all at the touch of a button. As far as I can see, there are only two things missing from the navigation repertoire of the smartphone. One is radar, but even that one is in the process of being solved with software that allows the output from a radar antenna to connect via a Bluetooth link directly to your phone, so that the radar picture is displayed on the screen. Not only

PHONES, TABLETS AND COMPUTERS

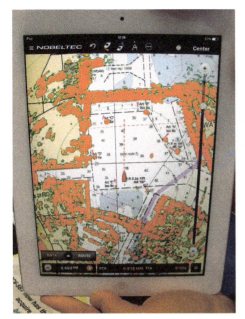

The radar picture on a tablet transmitted by Bluetooth

does the radar display come up on the phone display but you can control it from there as well. This radar system works in much the same way as a full size radar, although the tiny display can make it very hard to identify what you are seeing, particularly the weak returns from small craft With the Bluetooth link you can walk around the boat and still see your radar picture, although as with any radar picture, you need to relate it to what you identify visually outside.

The second thing missing from the smartphone capability is its use as a depth sounder but even this could be possible in desperate circumstances by tying a piece of string around the phone and dropping it overboard! Everything else you might need for navigation is contained in the one small portable package, although AIS apps are not live AIS returns but those picked up at shore stations and re-broadcast.

Of course, its small size and portability does make it vulnerable. You might drop it, you might lose it, you might have a flat batery, is is not waterproof, or it might just stop working, leaving you vulnerable if you have put all your trust into this one unit.

Many have found reassurance in having each navigation requirement contained in a separate unit, so that if one fails, you still have the others to keep you going. I would be very nervous about entrusting all my navigational requirements to one smartphone package when out at sea but, as long as you are prepared to fall back on traditional navigation techniques if needed, you should be able to manage.

Perhaps the smartphone can be best employed as a back up to the conventional electronic navigation systems taking over from handheld GPS receivers, chart plotters and the like. It should work at least until the batteries run out if, if all your other onboard electrics have failed.

Let's now have a closer look at each navigational function that the smartphone can provide. This will give a better picture of what it can and cannot do. This information is also relevant to those who use a pad or tablet at sea.

Communications

You can make phone calls and send text messages using the smartphone wherever there is coverage by your network provider. If you want to get more sophisticated results

Smartphone charts and information displays

PRACTICAL NAVIGATION *121*

PHONES, TABLETS AND COMPUTERS

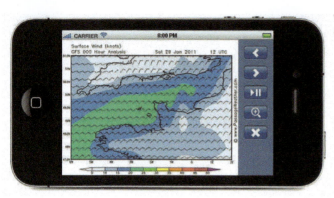

Weather information on a smartphone

then you will need at least the 3G level of coverage, which tends to be less extensive, particularly out at sea. For normal mobile phone coverage you can be pretty certain of receiving signal up to five miles offshore and in many areas up to ten miles, provided you are not sailing in a remote area, but after that it can be rather hit and miss. There will always be dead spots that the signal cannot reach, particularly along a rocky coastline lined with cliffs but these dead areas may only exist inshore.

Whilst there are detailed maps showing mobile phone coverage on land, there are none for sea areas, so the only way to learn whether reception might be available is the hard way, by trial and error. To a certain extent, the same applies to VHF radio, where, again, there is no guarantee of having coverage and being able to maintain communication with the Coastguard, particularly along coastlines with high cliffs and deep bays. In theory, even when using a smartphone, a VHF radio should still be considered essential for hearing distress messages and sending out your own and for getting hold of up to date marine weather forecasts and navigation warnings. Boaters are now frequently using mobile phones rather than VHF for routine matters such as organising a berth in a marina, and you certainly don't want to be using your marine VHF to book a table in a restaurant.

Many marine apps have the facility to simply tap on a port or marina on the chart display and instantly view the telephone number of many local facilities. One more

tap on the screen and the phone is ringing. If only navigation was as easy as booking a restaurant table or a marina berth.

GPS reception

GPS is the key to accurate position fixing and smartphones have an in-built receiver that can offer a position in latitude and longitude at all times. However, you will notice that your conventional chart plotter has its GPS antenna located outside the boat to ensure continuous reception. Your smartphone GPS antenna will presumably be based inside the boat most of the time, so you will need to check that the GPS works when you are inside, under cover. It may work close under the windscreen and it should have no issues on an open boat or on the flybridge but GPS reception is certainly something to check before you commit

A computer is almost an essential part of any chart table

122 PRACTICAL NAVIGATION

PHONES, TABLETS AND COMPUTERS

yourself to smartphone navigation.

Smartphone GPS systems tend to be comparatively weak and are usually just single channel receivers. This means they are only able to communicate with one satellite at a time, unlike the multi-channel GPS receivers that talk to each GPS satellite simultaneously. Single channel GPS receivers are likely to take longer to access the satellites on start-up but once up and running they should perform OK. It is worth noting that the GPS antenna in a phone is less likely to have anti-jamming technology built in.

As far as GPS accuracy is concerned, it is possible to download very cheap or free GPS status apps that will show your position, speed and course, etc. in numerical form, whilst also showing the accuracy level of the position shown. They offer no explanation of how this accuracy is determined but it can give you an idea of how good the GPS is. These apps also enable you to plot your position on paper charts if you want to simplify your mobile phone navigation.

I use the Pocket GPS World app, partly because it is free and partly because I like to see the accuracy level being offered, which always seems to be lower than what you might expect from GPS positioning using a dedicated marine receiver. When using my smartphone to navigate in narrow channels I have found that it will occasionally plot the position over land rather than in the channel so my advice is to keep a close watch on the plotted positions and to only use this type of electronic navigation in the open sea rather than for position-critical navigation.

Navigation apps

There is a wide range of navigation apps available for smartphones and tablets, and the range of what they offer is equally wide.

The main choice you need to make in selecting an app is between vector and raster charts, and this can come down to personal preference.

Vector charts tend to work better on the small screen because you can filter out much of the information that you don't need, but

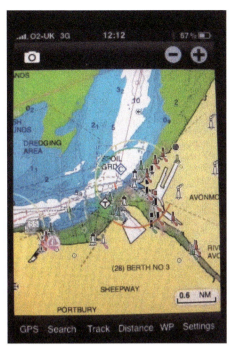

The chart detail on a smartphone is almost as good as on plotters

you need to be careful that you don't filter out vital information. The main suppliers here are Navionics and Jeppeson but there are others, particularly in the US where NOAA charts are widely used.

Raster charts are exact replicas of paper charts and the Imray app is good. Again, in the US, raster charts are also available.

Some of the available apps include weather maps and most have tidal information. When choosing, it's worth doing quite a bit of research to find the app that works for you.

I personally use the Navionics app, which I have found on of the best for both route planning and for navigation itself. This offers most of the facilities that are found on mainstream chart plotters compressed onto the small screen of a mobile phone. There is worldwide chart coverage and you simply pay to download the app that is relevant to the area that you plan to sail in. You can get chart coverage of the whole of the UK and

PRACTICAL NAVIGATION **123**

PHONES, TABLETS AND COMPUTERS

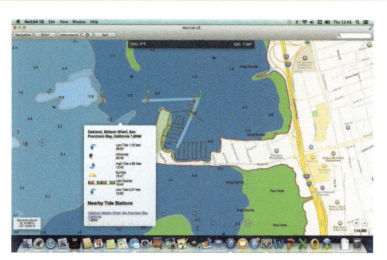

A laptop chart display that focuses as much on the land as the water

Northern Europe for the price of a couple of bottles of wine. However, the compact size of the screen can make things a bit difficult, particularly if you have large fingers. The system is operated via a touch screen and you might need to make two or three attempts when trying to set a waypoint before you get it in the place that you want.

When you are plotting a route, you need to take extra care that the route you have chosen is free from dangers by expanding the scale and carefully studying the route in detail. I found it is all too easy to set the waypoints and then find that the chosen route passes over a rock or shoal that does not show up well on the small screen. With smartphone navigation, you do need to be extra vigilant and check that the route you have selected is safe.

Plotting a course

On some systems like Navionics, waypoints are set by simply tapping the screen in what you believe is the right location. A finger is a fairly crude pointer when you are looking at it in relation to the screen size so it is not easy to set waypoints accurately. However, they are easy to adjust, again by simply touching the waypoint and dragging it to where you want it to be. It took me five minutes to plot a route involving ten waypoints but it then required the same time again to check it afterwards.

Once plotted, all you need to do is keep the 'own ship' icon on the course line to follow the route with suitable course adjustments being made to maintain the chosen route. You can set the track plotting mode so as to have a record of where you have been and you will get a heading vector and speed read out, provided that you are doing more than five knots. This might prove a handicap for sailboats, for which the heading vector is particularly useful as a means of seeing where you are going in relation to the plotted route.

With most of the apps that I have tested you can get the tidal height and current direction as well as the general chart information. You need to spend some time playing with the system you choose as they don't always come with instructions. Because you may not be boating, nor using the apps, every day of the week, you may forget how to use some of the more subtle features and so learning has to start again. Smartphone navigation is wonderful but I still find myself reluctant to put my full faith in the system and totally rely on it.

AIS

It is not possible to get a direct read from the AIS transmitters on board the ships around you using a smartphone but the next best thing is a marine traffic app such as Ship Finder. With these apps you can go to any

PHONES, TABLETS AND COMPUTERS

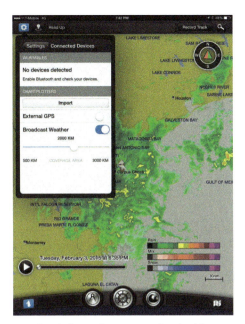

Weather information on a netbook; this one only shows rainfall

location around the world and you can see the position of the vessels that are transmitting AIS signals. Tap on a ship icon and it will show you all the details of the selected boat, including its size, destination, course and speed. Whilst useful, this function is certainly no substitute for a full-blooded AIS installation. It will not send out signals to other ships to say where you are, so this version of AIS may be less of interest as a serious navigation tool and more as a means of identifying a ship that you sight out at sea and gaining some idea of where it might be heading. However, AIS systems do require an internet connection, which can be a challenge out at sea unless you use expensive satellite connections.

Compass

Most smartphones have a built-in compass but there are also a number of alternative compass apps available. The standard display shows both an analogue and a digital readout of your heading and having checked this at sea, it seems to be reasonably accurate to within 5°. It is hard to get better accuracy because the heading shown on the display is the direction that the iPhone is pointing and it is difficult to get this lined up exactly with the bow of the boat; it takes just a slight movement of the phone to change the heading by several degrees. This compass display is based on analysis of subsequent GPS positions so there will be a small delay in the updating of the headings shown. I would hate to have to steer a boat using a phone compass but as an emergency back-up it works and it could help to get you home.

Although the primary compass display is given as a true course, you can set the phone to show magnetic headings, where the variation is automatically added to the true heading depending on your location around the world.

Alarms

A smartphone is a wonderful device because it can give you so much information in such a small package, but this is actually a problem. The worry is that with time you will cease checking whether the smartphone is giving good quality navigation information.

The biggest concern is the quality of the GPS position information because so much of your navigation will depend on this. I used an app that tells you the quality of the GPS fix but it means switching over to this at frequent intervals. It would be much better to have an automatic system that throws up an alarm when the GPS position is poor. I am sure this will come with time. It would also be good to have other alarms that could be set, such as warnings about the approach to shallow water and cross track error alarms when you are drifting away from the set route.

Battery life

Battery life is a particular concern when using a phone for navigation. The smartphone is very power hungry and the battery will soon drain if you have the display switched on for long periods whilst navigating. It is possible to get phone

PRACTICAL NAVIGATION 125

chargers that plug into car-type cigarette lighter charger units. These should keep the battery working for as long as you need it and are now becoming an essential part of any boat's facilities for charging phones, tablets, etc. However, they are not waterproof, so you may be restricted in terms of where they can be installed. Another option is to carry supplementary batteries that can be connected to the phone but, again, you come up against the waterproofing problem. You can purchase mounts and protective cases for phones, some of which are waterproof and allow the phone to be mounted in an exposed cockpit. However, whilst you can make the phone watertight with a case, you probably can't do the same for the charging system. This could restrict the use of the phone to inside the boat but, as mentioned previously, this may stop you getting a GPS signal. It is all a bit of a vicious circle and personally, I would not rely on a phone system as my primary means of navigation. Also, remember that using your phone for navigation could be data hungry which could be a problem if you are on a limited use tariff.

Tablets

Tablets (including iPads) offer much the same technology that is found in a smartphone. From a navigational point of view, the best thing about them is that they offer a larger screen, which can make them more viable as a navigation tool. The larger display makes it a lot easier to find your way around the systems that you install. Everything is touch screen, as with the phone, but you are still faced with the problems of maintaining the charge and keeping the item away from water. The larger display may tempt you to use your tablet as a mainstream navigation system and it can fulfil this function but, again, I would be reluctant to do this because of the possibility of loss of GPS signal and the risk of water damage.

In time it may become possible to connect smartphones and tablets to an outside GPS antenna in order to obtain a more reliable signal, and to connect them to a reliable waterproof power supply but then you are almost back to using a dedicated navigation system. Advances are being made all the time and we now have Bluetooth connections that allow radar information to be displayed on your phone or tablet, so perhaps the same technology could be used for connection to a GPS antenna.

In the meantime, do consider the risks and think about keeping your dedicated marine system, even if it is only a handheld GPS.

Summary

All of these navigation systems have a role to play in creating a good and reliable approach to electronic navigation but when deciding what to use you must always consider the worst-case scenario, because at sea you are out there on your own. Of course you can manage if the electronics go wrong, as we have shown in earlier chapters, but try to minimise the risks and understand the limitations of what are primarily land-based systems. We are in a sort of transition period where the convenience, capability and cost of these portable units has to be balanced against the reliability and robustness of the dedicated units.

13 The future

Having an idea of where navigation will be heading in the future can help you to decide what you should invest in, in terms of equipment and systems. At present the choice can be bewildering, with manufacturers vying to add the most bells and whistles to their systems and outdo their competitors. Behind all this so-called development are the bare bones of navigation systems, such as radar, position fixing, and underwater detection. So will we see any changes to these basic systems that could affect the way we navigate?

Radar

Radar has changed considerably since its early days. The size of the unit has been greatly reduced and it has switched from a combined mechanical/electronic system to a fully electronic one. This has enabled the returned signal from the radar transmission to be processed by sophisticated software, which gives a clearer picture. The relatively new broadband radar does not transmit pulses like conventional radar but, instead, sends out a continuous signal on varying frequencies, identifying targets by changes in frequency. It sounds simple but the technology is complex and the end result is a system that has a much higher accuracy at close range but a reduced overall range. At present the jury seems to be out about which system is the best. My view is that with the availability of GPS position fixing, you rarely need to use radar ranges beyond 20 miles, so the improved discrimination of the broadband radar gives it an advantage. However, this needs to be balanced against the fact that the broadband radar will not trigger Racons and some other radar target enhancing systems, which could be a drawback when navigating in fog.

We are also seeing the emergence of 3G and 4G radars from various manufacturers. These use the traditional pulsed radar but have advanced software to process the returned signal, enabling the system to distinguish between wave or rain returns on the radar and weak radar returns from boat or buoy targets. The 3G and 4G terms can be confused with mobile phone signals, but tend to reflect the standard of the software rather than anything else. Big ship radars use highly complex software to do this job and enable the detection of small craft targets with a higher degree of certainty. Small boat radar systems may develop in a similar way. It does, naturally, cost considerably more to develop advance software but by widening the market to cover small boat radars, the cost per unit could be reduced considerably.

So it looks likely that we will see better performing radars in the future, but the biggest advance would be the development of a system that combines the rotating radar antenna with other detectors like the low light camera and thermal imaging camera described in Chapter 11. Think of the possibilities that could emerge! What one of these detection systems might miss, another could find and once a target was detected it

A horizontal large scale chart plotter that acts and looks like the paper chart

THE FUTURE

could be identified and confirmed by the other systems. For this idea to work, the visual detection offered by the two camera systems would need to be changed into digital detection that could be matched to the radar picture. Such a system would allow much greater confidence in detection and greatly reduce the chance of small targets going undetected.

Accurate position fixing

This has been transformed by the advent of GPS and its sister satellite systems. Knowing where you are to an accuracy of 20 metres should be more than adequate for most practical navigation purposes but this accuracy can be increased in areas where there is differential GPS (DGPS) available. To achieve the 3 to 4 metre accuracy that can be found with DGPS, the GPS derived position is measured at an accurately known location. The difference between the two readings is the GPS error; this is transmitted out to sea and automatically applied to the GPS position on the receiving vessel. Bringing the accuracy of a position down to just a few metres could give a lot more confidence when using GPS for navigation in a harbour but do we need to achieve such a high level of accuracy and do we have charts able to match it? To make the information useable, you would need to know the accuracy of the chart to which the position is being applied but few charts, either paper or electronic, are likely to have this level of accuracy. Use of DGPS positions could lead navigators to place too much reliance on the given position, whereas the small area of doubt that is incurred with the normal 20-metre accuracy allows for the application of a suitable degree of caution. We have to remember that a position in latitude and longitude is not much use unless it can be plotted on a chart and related to the surroundings.

We have already talked about the possibility of a terrestrial-based backup for GPS and this is developing slowly. It has become much more important now that virtually all transport systems rely on GPS in one way or another and a failure in GPS positioning could have serious consequences. eLoran is the terrestrial-based system favoured for development at present. It would work for most marine and aircraft requirements, however, the fact that it probably will not be suitable for fitting into portable devices, such as mobile phones, could stall its introduction. If eLoran does go ahead, you could find your navigation devices heading off in two different directions: one followed by larger fixed receivers with the space to incorporate the relatively large eLoran antenna as a back-up; the other by portable devices unable to accommodate the back-up system. Combined GPS and eLoran receivers are already available commercially but the extra expense is unlikely to make them viable for small craft for some time yet.

Sensors

Truly new developments in electronic systems for yachts are largely related to the development of new sensors. The transformation of the echo sounder from downward-looking to forward-looking is an example of this. Fishing boats have been using this type of sensor for many years to track or detect shoals of fish but its use in the leisure market is still in its infancy. We are likely to see ever-greater refinement of sonar

Real-time tidal streams shown on the navigation display

THE FUTURE

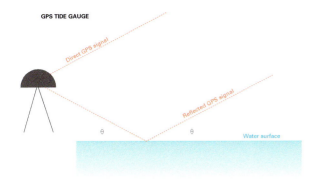

The way in which a GPS tide gauge could work measuring the difference between the real and reflected signals arrival

technology to improve underwater detection and much of this is already available for specialised applications. However, with sonar readings generally acting as a back up for other sources of information, the benefits are not so easy to see, which, in turn, is reflected in the slow take up of these advanced sonar systems. If the cost came down, sonar technology could find a wider application, although this may be superseded by a greater trust in what underwater information is contained within charts. Problems could arise if you find yourself with conflicting information from the chart and the sonar, raising the question of which to trust.

In aircraft, the problem of which information to trust when faced with conflicting readings from a multitude of sensors is overcome by the use of three position fixing systems; if the readings differ, go with the majority. This is the sort of technology that will be required before we put total faith in electronics. In the meantime, a marine craft has the advantage of being able to stop and work things out if there is doubt, something an aircraft cannot do.

The introduction of tiny chips now used in equipment like smart watches that can access the GPS signal will open up the way for virtually any electronic system to receive GPS signals. But this GPS chip needs some way of accessing the GPS signal. Currently, all of the electronic navigation equipment produced by one manufacturer can be linked together so that it is fully integrated and the formerly independent units can 'talk' to each other and share information. This enables a wider use of the available information and even the potential to obtain new types of information, as seen in Chapter 8. Computers can use the basic information provided by the sensors to calculate much more sophisticated data. The use of this type of processing will increase but it must be done in such a way that the basic information is still available if there is a break in the sharing link and it is important that each individual sensor is still able to act as a stand-alone unit. There must also be some reassurance that the quality of the basic information on which all the electronic calculations are made remains of a suitably high quality to justify the processing results. The computer-related phrase 'garbage in, garbage out' very much applies in this situation.

Displays can now be tailored to suit different cruising situations

THE FUTURE

A single display can show a wide variety of alternative information

GPS, tides and depths

An innovative new use of GPS is presented by the proposals for a GPS tide gauge. This would involve matching the GPS signal that follows a straight path into the onboard antenna with the signal that is reflected to the antenna from the surface of the sea. The reflected path takes a slightly longer route and the difference in the time taken can be used to calculate the height of the tide. It may only work in calm water and is more likely to be used by harbour authorities as a means of obtaining real time tidal information but it demonstrates yet another use for the ubiquitous GPS signal. A further tide-related possibility is for the depths shown on electronic charts to be adjusted automatically for the tidal variation so that they show real time depths.

In place of hardwired connections we are increasingly seeing use of ethernet or Bluetooth connections, just like those used for your home or office computer. This technology makes it possible to control your autopilot, or even the throttles, when you are some distance away from them. I am not convinced of the validity of this type of control because it seems somewhat dangerous to give navigators the potential to control their boat when away from the helm and thus from the lookout. Although much of the technology being developed would appear to give the impression that visual navigation is a thing of the past, it is vital to remember that the lookout is a legal requirement and that even with cutting edge systems at your disposal, the information gained by looking from the wheelhouse window remains the most dependable. It continues to be essential for successful navigation.

Validating electronic information

One development long overdue is a means of checking the validity of the electronic information presented to the navigator. In most cases, at present, you have to make you own judgement about the quality of the available information but it would be nice to see it validated electronically so as to know how much trust you should put in it. Navigating has always been about checking the quality of the available information but we are starting to lose sight of this and being encouraged to take information for granted.

Automatic navigation

At present we find ourselves at something of a crossroads in navigation. The technology is there for fully automatic navigation: just tell the boat where you want to go and it will arrive at its destination. We are seeing this with cars too, but the clear definition of roads makes both navigation and collision avoidance much simpler.

A display showing a wide variety of display and control features that is perhaps too complex for easy use

THE FUTURE

Another display that automatically changes to suit the navigation mode

At sea, the technology is there for basic automatic navigation. The main weakness in that scenario is collision avoidance but already there are ship systems that carry this out automatically. Major work is going on to develop unmanned ships. This would offer big savings in crew costs and, the argument goes, improvements in safety because it is human error that is largely responsible for accidents at sea. It is mainly the tried and tested Colregs that stand in the way of these unmanned ships and these would have to be seriously amended before this scenario becomes a reality. For boats the cost of electronic systems and their back-ups would probably be prohibitive and for many yachts crew costs are not a major factor.

Ultimately, do we go to sea in order to sit back and relax and let the boat take care of itself? For me, setting out on a voyage at sea is a challenge and a welcome contrast to life on land, where you are governed by so many rules and regulations that there is a distinct loss of freedom of action and even thought. At sea you shake off these shackles and your actions are more or less governed by nothing more than the Colregs and common sense. With this freedom comes responsibility and this includes being responsible for the safe navigation of your boat. Good navigation is still a combination of skill and art, despite the advances in electronic technology, and getting it right can give a level of satisfaction that in itself constitutes a key motivation for going to sea.

14 Equipment and installation

Choosing the right electronic navigation equipment, and installing it so that it is easy to use, can make a huge difference to the pleasure and effectiveness of your navigation.

Most decisions as to what equipment is installed and where are made by boat designers and builders. Generally you must simply take what is on offer rather than being able to tailor the navigation station to your requirements.

Unfortunately, many designers and builders do not have a great deal of experience as regards the type of equipment and location that is likely to work best for the boat. The chosen installation, therefore, tends to be governed by what looks good, what is most convenient to install and what is most competitively priced. To lay out a paper chart you may have to resort to the cabin table as it is the only flat space available, whilst electronic systems tend to be fitted where there is convenient space rather than where is best sited for operation in difficult navigational scenarios.

Having the radar and chart pictures side by side is a good way of presenting information

Even electronic systems themselves are designed for general use on as many different boats as possible, rather than being adaptable for use in specific navigation scenarios. Wouldn't it be wonderful if you could, say, switch electronic displays into fog mode or sailing mode so that the information displayed was matched to the navigation situation you were having to cope with?

Sun reflections on the display on a motorboat can make them difficult to read

SELECTING EQUIPMENT AND INSTALLATION

Here the focus of the installation is on the engine dials not the navigation displays

This central display works well when it is a two man helm

Again the engine monitoring panels take priority rather than the navigation displays

The radar and the chart would be better close together so that direct comparisons can be made

Specifying the equipment

Whilst you may not have much say in the location of the equipment if it was determined when the moulds were designed, you may be able, at least, to specify the equipment you want and this could go some way towards creating a more tailored installation. If you are one of the lucky ones starting from scratch or replacing out of date electronics, you will have a wide range of systems to choose from. When making a choice, bear in mind that what might look good and simple to operate when you see it at a boat show may not stand up to the challenge of use on a dark night, in rough seas.

What you need is a piece of equipment that is both simple to operate and intuitive to use. Remember that if you use your boat just once a fortnight or less, it can be a learning process each time you go on board, requiring you to refresh your memory as to how the electronic systems work and how to find the information you want. Once, when I was navigating by sight on a racing yacht, the fog came down and we had to switch to an electronic chart system that I was not familiar with. We didn't manage to win that race...

The trend towards equipment that is operated by touch screens means that you need easy finger access to the display, and it should, therefore, be within easy reach of the helm. The same could be said for push button operated equipment but this may come with the option of fitting a remote control panel that can be installed where it is easy to reach, thus enabling you to locate the display itself where it is most convenient and visible. In addition to push button and touch screen systems there are hybrid systems, combining both functions, to which the same considerations apply. It is not a good idea to mount any unit directly in front of the

PRACTICAL NAVIGATION *133*

SELECTING EQUIPMENT AND INSTALLATION

Controls that are part-push button and part-screen controlled

A remote control unit can be positioned for easy use from the helm

Push button controls

The type of button used can make a difference to ease and effectiveness of use.

Shape

Buttons that are flat across the top or located under a smooth waterproof membrane can be difficult to use accurately when the boat is moving about. Your finger can easily slide off the selected button or even push the wrong one if you are jolted whilst operating the unit. The best type of push button has a convex top for your finger to rest in, meaning that there is a better chance of your finger staying in contact with it.

Illumination

You may be using a push button display at night, so it is important to have some form of button illumination. Electronic equipment often has a bright pinpoint light to indicate that there is power in the unit. This can be very irritating at night and a bit of sticky tape can come in handy to blank out the light. When you are purchasing new equipment, try to evaluate it in the dark to see how it will stand up to use at night or in poor weather. Can you operate the controls effectively? Is the night display adjustable or is there just one bright or dim setting? Do you need to get the torch out every time you want to adjust the equipment? There is no doubt that touch screen displays are better for night use because the controls are always illuminated on the display.

steering wheel on a motorboat because you will find it hard to reach the controls over the wheel. On a sailboat, the steering pedestal may be a suitable location for installation of devices, although the wheel can still intrude here. Larger sailboats have the navigation station down below, where there is more freedom to arrange the displays, but whatever the boat size or type, easy and comfortable access to the controls or screen is important.

When choosing a location for the equipment, try to visualise what it will be like to operate it when on board a boat that is moving about in waves or, in the case of a sailboat, heeled over to one side. If you are trying to steer the boat as well as operate the electronics, you will have you hands full, so easy access and operation is important. What seems logical and easy in the warmth of a boat show might be very different on a wild night at sea, which is the time when you will be most reliant on the electronic navigation information.

Electronic displays that do not distract from the view out of the window

SELECTING EQUIPMENT AND INSTALLATION

A full push button control unit

A full touch screen display that works well in harbour but which can be challenging to use in rough seas

Touch screen displays

Touch screen displays are becoming ever more popular on boats. The omnipresence of touch screen devices in daily life means that many of us are well accustomed to their use. However, on a moving boat it can be difficult to use a touch screen well, as it may be tricky to touch the right icon on the display or to accurately position a waypoint. On some systems you may be able to overcome this by expanding the range on the display in just the same way as you do on a phone.

Some touch screens can become less responsive if they get wet, meaning that they may not be the best solution for a display mounted in an open cockpit. The responsiveness of a wet touch screen can depend on the type of water that it has come into contact with; apparently the worst is warm fresh water, i.e. rain. Before you purchase a system, check the likely effects on it of contact with water; the cockpit on a sailboat can be one of the wettest places on earth in rough conditions, which is exactly when you will want to be able to use the equipment easily. If you are wearing gloves, you will not be able to work the touch screen without removing them, unless you are using special gloves designed for use with touch screen technology. The use of touch screens for navigation at sea is still in its infancy but, in light of their ubiquity in everyday life, it is likely that they will be here to stay.

Widescreen formats

Virtually every display on the market today has a wide screen, where the width is greater than the height. This follows the trend seen on TVs and computers but it is not the necessarily the best format for navigation. With radar you want the maximum view ahead possible and with a head-up display, which is the norm for small craft, the wide screen reduces this view. You can usually move the centre of the screen downwards to expand the view ahead but essentially the widescreen format is something that we must learn to live with.

Glare and reflections

When choosing where to install equipment, it is useful to remember that a display will reflect sunlight, making it very difficult to see

Touch screen control can be difficult in lively seas

PRACTICAL NAVIGATION **135**

SELECTING EQUIPMENT AND INSTALLATION

Bright sunlight makes it impossible to read the electronic display

what is on the screen. Sailboat cockpits often have the displays mounted horizontally on the pedestal, in front of the steering wheel, which is probably the worst location in terms of exposure to sun. A vertical screen is probably the best but it is rarely easy to achieve a screen at this angle on board, so you will usually end up with a display angled at perhaps 20° from the vertical. This should still work reasonably well but any more than that and you are likely to have issues with the sun and even at 20° it might be a good idea to attach a hood at the top to reduce the glare.

Sun reflection can be equally problematic inside the wheelhouse of a motor cruiser. Here, problems can arise when the sun shines through the windscreen from above. Again, it may be possible to solve the problem by fitting a hood to the top of the display, or the equipment could be recessed into the dashboard rather like in a car. At times, even light coloured clothing can cause problematic reflections onto the displays. A good solution is to install an adjustable display whose angle can be altered to suit the conditions; this could be particularly valuable on a sailboat.

On motorboats with wheelhouses the displays are invariably mounted on the dashboard in front of the helm. You may have single or twin displays and there is an increasing trend to add a third display to monitor all the equipment on board. This may also be used to control items such as generators, lights and the flaps through a touch screen interface. It is not ideal to have all this information on the dashboard because when navigating at sea you want simplicity and minimum distraction. When something goes wrong, the alarms are much more likely to give the first indication of any fault than a display. The ideal layout is probably two displays, one for the chart and one for the radar, although you can sometimes have these two features combined into a single display with a split screen.

On sailboats the trend is to have a single display in the cockpit at the helm or perhaps two displays on larger yachts with two helms. The exposed position means that the units must be fully watertight. They may also be slave displays that repeat the information shown on the main display, located at the chart table below.

Let's now look at the requirements for individual pieces of electronic equipment.

Radar

Radar is one of the oldest electronic navigation instruments and it has advanced dramatically since it became digital. Most electronic equipment used on board gives quite precise information but with small boat radars you have to sometimes coax the information out of the equipment. You do need experience in order to identify what you see on the display, so getting the right radar for the job can be important. There are two main things to look for when selecting a radar:

Display

A large display will help you to spot and identify some of the smaller targets much more clearly and it will make it easier to get a clear picture of the targets. The displays associated with some small boat radars are simply too small to offer a clear picture, especially problematic when you consider that it is on these smaller craft that the motion of the boat is likely to be most intense and you will, therefore, have most need of a clear, easy to interpret picture.

SELECTING EQUIPMENT AND INSTALLATION

Antenna

The larger the antenna, the better the distinction between targets that are close together. It is mainly the beam width that suffers as the antenna gets smaller. A reasonable small boat radar will have a beam width of 3 to 5° and this would be associated with an antenna of perhaps 24 inches. On one recently introduced small boat radar the beam width is a massive 7.5° which means that any targets roughly on the same range within this sector angle will appear as a single target. This could make it hard to distinguish between buoys and nearby small craft, whilst harbour entrances between piers might not show up until you are quite close due to the wind beam angle picking up both piers at the same moment. The length of individual pulses from the radar will determine how clearly you can distinguish between targets that are on the same bearing but at different ranges. Pulse length tends to be automatically adjusted by the radar with a shorter pulse when you are using the radar on shorter ranges and a longer, more powerful pulse for longer ranges.

Adjusting the radar

Most radars are self-adjusting so when you switch them on, the settings such as gain, sea and rain clutter are automatically adjusted for the range and conditions. You can usually override these automatic settings; useful when you are trying to find a small target in rough seas. Unfortunately the radar returns from waves can be just as strong as the returns from small craft, so in rough seas you want to be able to fine-tune the strength of the sea clutter returns in the hope that the small targets might show up. With software-based systems it may take a few keystrokes to find the manual settings for these items although some of the more sophisticated radars have an automatic system that checks all the radar returns and highlights those that remain constant. This can help you to differentiate between boat targets and the more random returns from waves. This topic is covered in more detail in Chapter 6 (Collision Avoidance) and is something to bear in mind when selecting equipment.

Overlaying the radar picture onto the chart display can be useful when you are trying to identify fixed targets such as buoys. It can also be useful to be able to view two radar pictures side by side. In poor visibility it can help to have one display on perhaps a 2-mile range for collision avoidance manoeuvres and the other on a 5-mile range for the early detection of targets. There are a wide variety of features incorporated into software-based radars, so it should be possible to pick out the ones that you think are important. It is worth remembering that although radar is principally used for collision avoidance, it can offer a useful back-up for navigation should the electronic chart or GPS fail. Features such as a variable range and bearing marker can be very useful when it comes to navigation and also have their role to play in collision avoidance. Another good reason for installing the radar in a place where it is easy to use.

Radar is changing and the familiar rotating antenna that has been its hallmark, whether it is an open antenna or one enclosed in a radome, is being replaced by solid state systems. These new antenna are thought to offer greater reliability because there are no moving parts and it is also claimed that they offer better discrimination at shorter ranges, so they may be worth considering for your boat.

A low radar antenna means that the signal can be blocked by people standing on the flybridge

SELECTING EQUIPMENT AND INSTALLATION

Electronic chart

The electronic chart consists of three main components, which must come together if the system is going to work:

- Hardware, which is basically a computer with dedicated software
- Cartography, which is the actual charts, and often located on a memory stick or card
- The GPS, for positional information. The GPS needs an antenna mounted in an open position outside so that it can pick up signals from all around the horizon. On a fibreglass boat it may be possible for the antenna to work from inside but the signal will be weaker. You may find the GPS antenna incorporated into the main unit on some electronic chart systems.

Electronic chart hardware

Finally, there is the electronic chart hardware. Here, as with the radar, biggest is best. There are some tiny electronic chart displays on the market, mainly designed for sports boats, small sailboats and RIBs, where dashboard space may be limited. There is no doubt that they work just as well as their bigger brothers but the small screen size can make it very hard to read and interpret the display, particularly when the boat is moving about in waves. It is small craft that really need the bigger display but cost and space have to be factored in against usability. Small displays get even smaller if the available screen area has to be split and shared with a radar or echo sounder display. So when choosing electronic chart equipment, go for the biggest unit your pocket and dashboard can accommodate.

Cartography

This can contain all sorts of extra information, such as satellite overlays (for example, Google Earth) that enable you to get an aerial view of the area. You can even get the equivalent of Street View to obtain horizontal pictures of a port you are approaching. The underwater contours can also be displayed in a variety of ways, perhaps as a three dimensional picture. However, all of these features can be a distraction from the actual job of navigating. They may be useful in some circumstances, perhaps when passage planning, but for navigation at sea, the tried and tested flat chart display is hard to beat. It relates much more clearly to the paper chart, making cross-referencing simple. Bear in mind that overcomplication can lead to errors, so keep it simple.

RASTER AND VECTOR CHARTS

There are two types of electronic chart, raster and vector:

Raster charts are simply an electronic scan of the existing paper chart. This gives a great picture of the chart but whilst you can expand and contract the picture, use and manipulation of the chart information is limited.

Vector charts are digital versions of the paper chart. Every feature of the paper chart is faithfully recorded and the chart information can be manipulated so that, for instance, you can set up a warning if, for example, your yacht goes inside a 10 metre sounding line on the chart. Buoy lights can also be set up to flash on the screen in their true sequence. It is vector charts that have truly unleashed the potential of electronic chart systems. It is also vector charts that are subject to the bells and whistles treatment of the manufacturers and you may well find yourself with access to information that you never even knew you wanted.

When using vector charts, bear in mind that if the scale is contracted to accommodate a wider area, you can lose some of the detail on the chart and features such as rocks and buoys may disappear. Some chart systems have a declutter control that simplifies the picture in crowded waters but beware of exactly what is being removed.

Autopilot

Although not strictly speaking a navigation tool, the autopilot is one of the most useful bits of equipment on board. Essentially, it holds the yacht on a pre-set course so that

SELECTING EQUIPMENT AND INSTALLATION

This electronic display is not well placed for either steering position

An autopilot with a rotary course control is best

you don't have to steer manually, freeing you up for look out and navigation and rendering navigation at night and in poor visibility much easier. The steady course of the autopilot will stabilise the radar picture, which will make it much more useful for collision avoidance. The autopilot can also be useful when entering harbour; I find that if you steer on autopilot, you can simply set the course and the autopilot will hold it until you want to make another change, thereby freeing you up to concentrate on where you are going.

Controls

In order to obtain the maximum benefit from the autopilot, choose one that has a knob, rather than a push button, to alter course. The push button is found on most cheaper systems and only allows you to alter course by increments of 1° or 10°, not a very subtle range. It is designed to work when you are altering course for collision avoidance at sea but for actually steering the boat the rotary knob control is much better. Here it can act as a substitute for the steering wheel, so the bigger the control knob the better. Unlike the steering wheel, when you let go of the autopilot knob the boat will hold that course until you make a further change.

Standby

Another feature that you should look for in an autopilot system is a prominent standby button that can be easily identified and enable you to disconnect the autopilot at a moment's notice. For use at night this standby button should also be clearly illuminated.

The autopilot can act as a compass and most systems provide a graphic display of the heading. Superimposed on this might be a wind indicator for sailboats, making it possible to get an idea of the possible sailing headings when you are close hauled. There is a tendency to put as much information as possible on the display but what you want is clear concise information when you need it, so simple is best.

Location

Locate the autopilot system within easy reach. Somewhere adjacent to the steering wheel is probably best. A portable, handheld system has now been introduced. This allows you to control the autopilot as you roam around the boat, which could be useful although you'll want to watch that you don't mislay the control somewhere!

Sounders and logs

Echo sounder

The echo sounder was one of the first electronic systems for boats and remains one of the most useful. The introduction of automatic plotting and positioning systems

PRACTICAL NAVIGATION **139**

SELECTING EQUIPMENT AND INSTALLATION

The AUTO button is the vital one for quickly disconnecting the autopilot

has somewhat altered its role and it is now used principally as a check on what the chart is showing. However, in navigation, checking information is everything, so the role of the echo sounder is still important.

Choose the location of the hull unit that sends out and receives the signals with care, making sure it is away from possible propeller interference and in a position where there is a clear water flow over the transducer. This transducer is never likely to be at the lowest point of the hull so make sure that you understand what the reading on the display is showing. It can be adjusted to show the depth from the surface of the water, the depth from the actual transducer or the depth below the keel. The depth from the surface is best for making chart comparisons but the depth under the keel can be useful if you are navigating in very shallow water.

Sophisticated sounder information can also be displayed on one of the navigation screens, usually in a split screen layout. This will show historical as well as real time depth information, which can be useful for navigation but is perhaps most valuable for the dedicated fisherman. Otherwise, both sounder and log information can be displayed on the main navigation display of integrated systems. On a racing sailboat a sounder that can give a verbal read out of the depth can be useful when you are approaching a tacking point on the edge of a bank.

Log

The log is still used on board, despite it now being possible to display speed from GPS readings. The two systems produce quite different readings as the log shows the speed through the water whilst the GPS shows the speed over the ground. The latter is probably more useful for navigation purposes but knowing the speed through the water can be vital for use of sailing instruments and as a means of measuring the effects of trimming the sails on a sailboat.

Sailing instruments

The sailing instruments are those that measure wind speed and direction and combine these readings with boat speed and other factors in order to show the apparent wind and other information that can help you sail your boat as effectively as possible. They have become very sophisticated and adept at showing the best sailing performance towards a waypoint. Not only do they help you to sail efficiently but also to

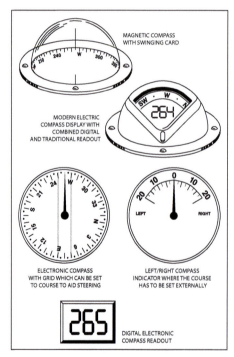

The variety of compass displays that can be found on yachts. Electronic compasses can usually be adjusted to give a true reading and it is important to know whether you are using magnetic or true.

SELECTING EQUIPMENT AND INSTALLATION

trim the sails effectively. The sailing information from these instruments may be displayed in high visibility displays on the mast or in the cockpit. They can be viewed as individual displays or combined onto a single larger screen. The cruising sailor may not be too concerned about squeezing the last drop of performance out of the sails but for the racing sailor these instruments are a vital piece of equipment.

AIS

The Automatic Identification System (AIS) is a development that can play an important role in collision avoidance. It operates through a VHF radio, either as an add-on to your existing radio or as a stand-alone unit and transmits data about your position, course and speed etc. This data is obtained from the GPS and can be automatically displayed on the screens of other vessels in the vicinity. The system, of course, works both ways and you will also be able to receive this data from other vessels. In theory, you should be able to obtain all relevant information on the other vessels around you, even their names and call signs, which can be a great help when taking avoidance action. The AIS information can be displayed on a small display on the AIS unit itself or, more usefully, it can be fed into the radar and/or the electronic chart display with a heading vector of the target to give you a better picture of what is going on around you.

It all sounds like a major advance but it does have its drawbacks. If every vessel had AIS on board, it would be fine but, currently, it is only compulsory on vessels over 300 tons. Then there are different class AIS units. Class A units are a requirement on ships and take priority. On yachts there is no requirement to fit AIS but those who choose to will usually fit the cheaper Class B unit, which should still make them identifiable on the displays of the big ships but only transmits every 30 seconds or so.

As discussed in Chapter 6, we have almost reached the stage where if you don't have a transmitting AIS fitted, you don't exist as far as the big ships are concerned. This could be very hazardous, especially in fog. The AIS unit is, therefore, starting to become an increasingly important piece of equipment for cruising yachts.

General

Power supply

As we make the switch from traditional to electronic navigation, the list of required electronic equipment grows longer. Not only does it become vital to get the layout and installation of the equipment right for easy use, but power supply is also key to reliable performance. Manufacturers of electronics make their equipment increasingly reliable but it all depends on a dependable power supply, a factor that is very much in the hands of the boat builder. Vital electronics ought to have the option of a back up supply from a dedicated battery if the main supply fails but I have yet to see this installed on any yacht.

Compatibility

With such a variety of electronic equipment, much of it needing to be integrated to enable the sharing of information, it pays to get all to the devices from one supplier to ensure compatibility. All the major suppliers of electronic navigation systems offer complete ranges of equipment. We are also seeing manufacturers from other fields of marine equipment providing integrated solutions. For example, some engine manufacturers now offer a sort of 'glass bridge', with navigation systems being thrown in alongside the engine monitoring. Communication specialists are also branching out into navigation electronics and there are still some specialist manufacturers of dedicated equipment. Add into this mix the use of phones, tablets and computers for navigation and you find yourself in a somewhat confusing world of possibilities. When choosing equipment and layouts, it pays to remember that boats operate in a very harsh environment where cheapest is rarely best.

Index

accelerometers, 116-17
Admiralty charts, 57-8
AIS
   apps, 120, 121, 124-5
   and collision avoidance, 64-5, 66, 70-71, 76
   failure & alarms, 69, 105
   lookout keeping, 64
   in poor weather, 66, 72, 76
   selection & installation, 141
alarms, 56-7, 69, 96, 105, 125
alternative ports & courses, 23, 25, 27, 28
anchorages, 19-20
angle of approach, 55
angles & directions, 93, 94
apps, 103, 120-25
ARPA (Automatic Radar Plotting Aid), 69-70
automatic distress call systems, 105
Automatic Identification System *see* AIS
automatic navigation systems, 130-31
autopilot, 48-9, 66, 85-6, 96
   alarms, 56, 105
   failure, 106-7
   fog & night navigation, 75, 77, 79, 80, 83
   remote control, 130
   selection & installation, 138-9, 140
   standby switches, 75, 77

batteries, 79, 103, 121, 125-6, 141
bays, 51-2, 89-91, 100
beacons, 41, 44, 47, 104, 127
bell & whistle signals, 78
blocking (of GPS), 9-10, 11, 12, 104-5, 123
Bluetooth, 120-21, 126, 130
breakwaters, 36, 42
buoys, 13, 37-40, 74
   in coastal areas, 46, 47
   harbour navigation, 36-40, 42, 44-5

cameras, 114-15, 127-8
cardinal marks, 38
chart datum, 15
chart plotters, 15, 25, 48, 49, 50, 96
   failure & alarms, 56, 103, 105
charts (general), 17-18, 23, 26, *see also* electronic charts; paper charts
circuit breakers, 102-3
Closest Point of Approach (CPA), 69, 70-71

coastal navigation, 46-59
   under power, 99-100
   under sail, 89-91
COG (course over ground), 84, 85, 94
collision avoidance, 60-71, 131, 137, 141
   in fog & night navigation, 74, 81
collision risk, 66-7
Colregs, 32, 49, 60-62, 66-9, 71, 131
   at night, 79, 81, 82, 114, 115
   in fog, 74-6, 78
Compass (Chinese system), 11
compasses, 49, 85, 94, 108, 115-16
   apps, 125
   fluxgate, 85, 115
   GPS, 85, 108, 115-16
   gyro, 116
   magnetic, 49, 107-8, 115
computers, 118-26, 129
conspicuous marks, 41, 55
course adjustment (night navigation), 81
course alteration under power, 98-9
course made good (CMG), 85
course over ground (COG), 84, 85, 94
course upwind, 91-2
CPA (Closest Point of Approach), 69, 70-71
crew, 32, 34, 53
   in fog, 73, 75, 76, 77
   see also visual lookout

danger buoys, 38, 39
dashboards *see* screens; wiring
Decca Navigator, 1, 12
depth sounding, 47-48, 55, 129, 130, *see also* echo sounders
directions, & angles, 93, 94
displays *see* screens
distances (cruise planning), 21-2, 23, 28, 30
distinctive features, 46, 55
dongles, 118
dopplers, 110

echo sounders, 13, 75, 111, 128-9
   coastal navigation, 47-8
   in fog, 75, 77
   harbour navigation, 42-3, 45
   selection & installation, 139-40
   and system failure, 109
   see also depth sounding

INDEX

electrics *see* power supply
electronic charts, 4-5, 15, 61, 119, 120, 128
   apps, 103, 123-4
   failure & alarms, 56-7, 103, 106, 109, 137
   fog & night navigation, 73, 78, 80-81, 82, 83
   and harbour navigation, 34, 36-7, 41, 43-4, 45, 83
   and passage planning, 18, 21, 23-5, 28-31
   selection & installation, 132, 138
   updates, 57-8
   vector & raster formats, 41, 123
   see also chart datum; chart plotters; screens
electronic logs, 94, 110, 117, 140
electronic navigation systems, 5-6, 85-7
   compatibility, 141
   failure & alarms, 2-3, 56-7, 102-9
   future developments, 127-31
   selection & installation, 132-41
   validating, 130
   weather routing, 32, 118
   see also screens
eLoran, 12, 106, 128
engine, checking on passage, 53
equipment
   future developments, 127-8
   selection & installation, 6, 132-41

failure
   and alarms, 56-7, 96, 105, 125
   of electrical supply, 102-3, 107
   of electronic systems, 102-9
fairway buoys, 38, 42, 44
fishfarms, 38, 44, 57
fishing marks, 96
flashing lights, 79, 80-81
fog, 72-8, 132, 133
   forecasting, 72, 74
   operation checklist, 75
   sound signals, 62, 73, 76, 77, 78
   types, 73-4, 75
fuel management, 28, 32, 34, 35, 53, 100-101

Galileo, 11
Global Positioning Systems *see* GPS
Glonass (Russian system), 11, 103, 106
Google Earth, 21
GPS, 2, 7-16, 85-6, 110, 128, 129
   accuracy & reliability, 2-4, 7, 12-13, 14-16, 128, 129
   antennae, 11-12, 13, 15, 104, 122-3, 126
   coastal navigation, 46, 48, 49, 50
   eLoran dual receivers, 106, 128
   failure & alarms, 56, 57, 103-7, 137
   fog & night navigation, 72, 73, 78, 83, 94
   GPS compasses, 108, 115-16
   harbour navigation, 37, 41, 43, 44, 45
   interference, 9-11, 12, 44, 104-5, 123
   landfall making, 55-6
   laptops, smartphones & tablets, 118, 121, 122-3, 125, 126
   tides & depths, 129, 130
Great Circle Route, 25

GRIB files, 117
ground stabilisation (MARPA), 70
gyros, 115, 116

harbours
   control signals, 36
   entering, 41-5, 73, 78, 82-3
   fog & night navigation, 73, 82-3
   leaving, 33-40, 73
   navigation checklist, 34, 36
headlands, 25, 52-4, 55, 90, 91, 99-100

IALA Buoyage System Region A, 39
Imray charts, 58
International Regulations for the Prevention of Collisions at Sea *see* Colregs
internet information sources, 20, 21, 28, 34, 57-9, 117
iPads, 126

jamming, 9-10, 11, 12, 44, 104, 123

landfall making, 55-6, 77-8, 92, 112
laptops, 118-20
latitude & longitude, 7, 15-16, 48, 105
lay lines, 95
leading lights & soundings, 13, 44
lee-bowing, 92
leeway, 93, 94
lighthouses, 41, 44, 46, 55, 80, 82
lights
   flashing & other signals, 79, 80-81, 82
   leading lights & soundings, 13, 44
   onshore, 55, 79, 82
   searchlights, 75, 76
   see also buoys; fog; navigation lights; night navigation; screens
log book record keeping, 53, 105, 109
logs, 94, 110, 117, 140
lookout keeping *see* sound signals; visual lookout
Loran, 1, 12, 106, 128

marinas, 19-20, 33-45
marks
   coastal navigation, 46, 47, 55, 96
   harbour navigation, 13, 37, 38, 39, 41, 44
   and passage planning, 23
   see also buoys; lights
MARPA (Mini-Automatic Radar Plotting Aid), 69-70
mileage (cruise planning), 21-2, 23

navigation apps, 123-4
navigation lights
onboard, 71, 75, 76, 78, 79, 82, 83
other vessels/onshore, 55, 79, 80-81, 82, 83
Navtex, 59
night navigation, 71, 78-83, 134
   operation checklist, 79
Notices to Mariners, 40, 57, 59

PRACTICAL NAVIGATION *143*

INDEX

offshore structure hazards, 55, 57, 58
offshore weather information, 117
open sea navigation, 52, 54-5
overtaking, 67-8

paper charts, 5, 15
  harbour navigation, 35, 41
  passage planning & course plotting, 17, 18, 23, 30, 106
  updates, 57-8
passage making
  checklist, 53
  open sea navigation, 54-5
  practising without electronics, 109
passage planning, 17-32
  last minute checks, 32
  legal requirements, 17
  navigation under power, 96, 97, 98, 100-101
  navigation under sail, 84, 85-9
  for night navigation, 80
  software, 119
peripherals, 110-117
phones, 103, 104, 120-26
position fixing, 1, 7-16, 111
  with smartphones, 122-3
position lines, 13
power boat navigation, 96-101
power supply, 79, 141
  failure, 102-3, 107
  to laptops & smartphones, 119, 121, 125-6
provisioning, 32

Racon beacons, 47, 127
radar, 1, 13-14, 34, 61, 137
  antennae, 76, 127, 137
  coastal navigation & landfall, 47, 50, 55-6
  and collision avoidance, 61-71, 137
  failure & alarms, 56, 69, 103, 105
  fog & night navigation, 73, 74-6, 79, 82, 83
  future developments, 120-21, 127-8
  selection & installation, 135, 136-7
  on smartphones & tablets, 120-21, 126
  see also screens
radio
  harbour, 34, 42, 73
  SSB, 117
  VHF, 34, 59, 64, 105, 122, 141
  weather forecasts, 20, 117
rain clutter, 63, 66, 69
regulations, 17, 32, 59, *see also* Colregs
remote control, 130-31, 133
Rhumb Line, 25
route planning, 19-20, 34

safety margins, 3-4
fog & night navigation, 73, 74, 75, 79
passage planning, 25, 26-7, 29, 30
sailboat navigation, 84-95
  fog & night navigation, 75, 77
sailboat performance parameters, 84
sailing instrument selection & installation, 140-41

satellites, 1-2, 7-9, 103-4, 106
screens, 61, 77, 89, 135-6
  decluttering, 25, 50
  dimming, 82
  electronic charts, 25, 45, 50, 135
  glare & reflection, 135-6
  push button displays & controls, 50, 77, 133-4
  radar, 63, 66, 68-71, 136-7
  sailing instruments, 94, 141
  size, format & onboard location, 126, 133-6
  sounders & logs, 111-12, 113, 140
  'three screens', 4-5, 61
  touch displays, 126, 133-4, 135
sea breezes, 90
sea clutter & wave returns, 68-9, 75, 137
sea stabilisation (MARPA), 70
searchlights, 75, 76
sensors
  future technology, 128-9
  masthead, 85, 86, 93, 117
shoals & shallows, 23, 38, 43, 47, 53, 111
shore lights, 55, 79, 82
signals
  fog, 62, 73, 76, 77, 78
  harbour control, 36
smartphones, 103, 104, 120-26
software developments, 28-9, 32, 85, 119, 127-31
SOG (speed over ground), 84, 85, 94
sonar sounders, 112-14, 128-9
sound signals (fog), 62, 73, 76, 77, 78
sounders, 110-114
  selection & installation, 139-40
  see also echo sounders
speed
  fast vessels & collision risk, 68
  safe speeds, 73, 74-6, 77, 78, 82-3
  under power, 97-8, 100-101, 140-41
  under sail, 85, 93, 94, 95
speed log, 110
speed over ground (SOG), 84, 85, 94
spoofing, 10, 11, 12, 104
steering, 49, 50-51, *see also* autopilot
stores & supplies, 32

tablets, 126
tacking, 91-2, 95
tides
  around headlands, 52-3
  GPS tide gauge, 130
  harbour entry, 45
  navigation under power, 99-100
  navigation under sail, 87, 92-3, 95
  passage planning, 21-2, 23, 28, 29, 119
timing (passage planning), 18
Traffic Separation Schemes (TSSs), 59
transducers, 111, 112, 113
transit bearings, 13
Transit satellite system, 1-2
transmitters affecting GPS, 105
triangular cruise, 19

underwater information, 128-9
updates, 57-9

VBM (Variable Bearing Marker), 66, 68
visibility, and collision avoidance, 60-62, 71, 81, 97, *see also* fog; lights; night navigation
visual lookout & navigation, 61-2, 64, 71, 96-7
   importance of, 4-5, 13, 33, 63, 115
   coastal navigation, 33, 46, 49, 67
   and electronic failure, 106-7, 108, 109
   fog & night navigation, 73, 74, 75, 76, 77, 80, 81
   in harbours, 33, 36, 43, 44

wave heights & lengths, 54, 97-8, 99, 117
wave returns & sea clutter, 68-9, 75, 137
waypoints
   passage planning, 23, 24, 25, 26
   when under way, 48, 86, 96, 103, 123-4
weather & forecasts, 6, 20-21, 23, 31-2, 117
wind, 6, 20, 22
   apparent wind, 84, 85, 86, 92, 93
   and autopilot, 49
   coastal navigation, 49, 51, 53-4, 89-90
   course upwind, 91-2
   and electronic weather routing, 32, 118
   forecasts, 20-21, 86-9, 117, 119
   gusts, 49, 53-4, 89
   harbour navigation, 42
   masthead sensors, 85, 86, 93, 117
   navigation under sail, 42, 84-95
   passage planning software, 119
wind triangle, 93-4
windfarms, 55, 57
windscreen view, 4-5, 13, 61-62, 63, 97, *see also* visual lookout
wiring, 102-3
World Geodetic System 1984 (WGS84), 15